HONG KONG

PORTRAITS OF POWER

HONG KONG

PORTRAITS OF POWER

Evelyn Huang & Lawrence Jeffery

With photographs by
Snowdon

WEIDENFELD & NICOLSON
LONDON

DEDICATION

To my husband Michael and my four children
Fiona, Anita, Jennifer and Gregory,
and the memory of my parents.
– Evelyn Huang

First published in Great Britain by
George Weidenfeld & Nicolson Ltd
The Orion Publishing Group
Orion House
5 Upper St Martin's Lane
London WC2H 9EA

British Library Cataloguing-in-Publication Data
A catalogue for this book is available from the British Library.

ISBN 0-297-83510-6

House editor: Richard Atkinson
Calligraphy by Irene Chu
Design by Design Revolution
Printed and bound in Hong Kong

ACKNOWLEDGEMENTS

We wish to thank the following individuals for their support
and encouragement: Amy Au, Joseph Chow, Irene Chu, George Eaton,
Norman Eckler, Professor Paul Evans, Professor Bernard Frolic,
James Ginou, Janese Kane, Wendy Kwok, Ellen Lam, Stephen Lam,
Pola Lee, Noëlle Lui, Deborah MacFarlane, Graham Piggott, Walter Stewart,
Barney Wan, Madeleine Webster, Pauline Yu, and special thanks
to Baroness Lydia Dunn and Anson Chan.

HONG KONG TODAY:

THE PRODIGAL RETURNS

THE TIME IS FAST COMING WHEN WE SHALL BE OBLIGED TO STRIKE
ANOTHER BLOW IN CHINA. THESE HALF-CIVILIZED GOVERNMENTS SUCH
AS THOSE IN CHINA, PORTUGAL, AND SPANISH AMERICA ALL REQUIRE
A DRESSING DOWN EVERY EIGHT OR TEN YEARS TO KEEP THEM IN ORDER.
THEIR MINDS ARE TOO SHALLOW TO RECEIVE AN IMPRESSION THAT WILL
LAST LONGER THAN SOME SUCH PERIOD AND WARNING IS OF LITTLE USE.
THEY CARE LITTLE FOR WORDS AND MUST NOT ONLY SEE THE STICK
BUT ACTUALLY FEEL IT ON THEIR SHOULDERS BEFORE THEY YIELD.

Lord Palmerston, Prime Minister, 1855

Li Ka-shing is the richest man in Hong Kong. On 1 July 1997, he becomes the richest man in China, and one of the most powerful men in a nation of 1.2 billion. He is running late. His executive assistant, one of only five he has had in his long career – and the first woman – calls to say he is caught in traffic in the tunnel running under Victoria Harbour from Hong Kong Island to the Kowloon mainland.

Lord Snowdon is pacing and anxious. This is the third and final sitting of the day, and the only subject to refuse categorically to sit for his portrait in anything but his customary blue suit, white shirt and tie. Snowdon thinks a white shirt and tie a disaster. The white shirt stops the eye from seeing much else. And glasses hide the eyes. And Li Ka-shing is late.

We have built a studio in a boardroom of the Royal Garden Hotel, which is part of the Kwok family empire. Walter, Raymond and Thomas Kwok, three brothers, operate Sun Hung Kai, the real estate and development company founded by their late father. In June 1993, *Fortune*

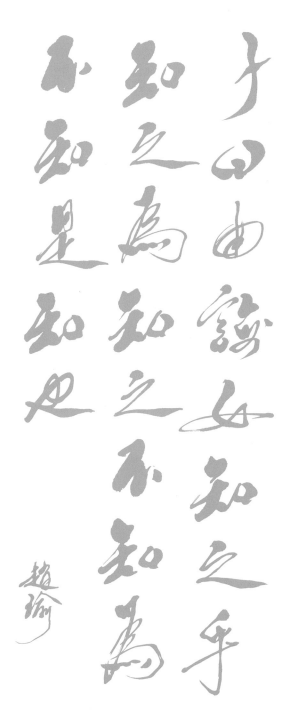

7

*Knowledge is
the ability to identify
the truth when you
see it and to admit it
when you do not.*

magazine listed the Kwoks as the fifty-third wealthiest family in the world, with a grand total of US $3.3 billion.

The past weeks have seen a parade of the most remarkable limousines deliver some of the wealthiest people in the world to the front door of this Kowloon hotel. It has not been easy. Egos to match bank accounts, and limousines – like Stanley Ho's cherry-red stretch Rolls-Royce – blocking traffic and drawing crowds. But Li Ka-shing is the king, or 'Superman' as he is called in Hong Kong. The man with the Midas Touch. And he's late.

Li arrives in the most elegant of all the limousines we will see. It is a dark teal-blue Nissan President sedan, with beige leather interior. Elegant, sleek, subtle, it slips out of the traffic and into the circular drive. The staff is prepared, security has been increased, but they remain discreet and at a distance. He smiles at us, steps out of his car and offers an apology as he extends his hand. He is relaxed, confident and comfortable with the attention his presence commands. He walks with a loping, loose-limbed gait; his voice is loud and clear, and his English impeccable. His voice cuts the air like a blade, but it is not a shout; there is no effort behind it, only force of personality. All eyes follow him. The lift waits for us. We enter and rise.

Li and Snowdon are of similar height and build. But they are from different worlds. The children of one stand twelfth and thirteenth in line for the British throne – old, Western nobility – while those of the other are heirs to one of the world's great fortunes – new, Eastern tycoonery.

They greet cordially, quietly. Nothing is said about lateness or inconvenience. Snowdon is already at work – his eyes scanning the face and clothes, his gentle humour working to relax his subject. Li is calm, but wary. Snowdon whispers some instructions about lighting and lenses to his assistant. He brings attention to Li's glasses, talks about how they draw the viewer's eye, how they hide the eyes and distort the face. Snowdon tells us that the only face that actually benefits from glasses belongs to John Major. Li nods, but does not smile. He will not be persuaded. He is firm, but polite. He says no one will recognize him without his glasses. No one has ever even seen him without his glasses. Suddenly, Snowdon reaches out and pulls the glasses away. There is a terrifying stillness. 'There,' says Snowdon, 'much better.' We wait. Seconds that seem lifetimes pass before Li smiles, shrugs and follows Lord Snowdon's invitation into the studio. Snowdon was right, as you will see on page 39; the portrait of Li with his glasses off *is* revealing.

This scene of mutual bafflement, a faint echo of historical collisions between the English and the Chinese, carried an almost corny symbolism, with Lord Snowdon, the former brother-in-law to the Queen, employing a modern and modified gunboat diplomacy, and Li Ka-shing, the Chinese tycoon, struggling to retain his dignity and control against the odds. He kept his dignity, but lost his point. Lord Palmerston would have understood; so would the Emperor Tao-Kuang (Dao Guang). We were to witness many other such scenes during the three weeks Lord Snowdon spent creating the remarkable portraits that illuminate the pages of this book.

This is a book about Hong Kong, and China, and the changes now shaking the Eastern and global economies, but a good deal of what we have to say can be understood most easily through the focus of this remarkable collection of men and women: Hong Kong's Super Group. These are the most powerful people in a city of power, mystery, wealth and, now, uncertainty. We selected these men and women because each represents an aspect or aspects of power in one of the most fascinating and important economies on earth at a time of change and challenge.

We are fast closing in on 1 July 1997, the day when Hong Kong is restored to the bosom of its Chinese family, a returning prodigal worrying whether the welcome will include the fatted calf, or a set of handcuffs. As you will see, the people on these pages have widely differing views of the prospect ahead, which range from dark pessimism, through modest expectation, to high hope. We do not, cannot, know which of them is right; we do know that, whatever happens, these are the key figures who will help to shape events after that crucial date.

There are a number of reasons for introducing these people, these portraits, at this time. In the first place, they are fascinating in themselves. These men and women are vastly rich, or immensely powerful, or both, and how they came to riches and power, and what they do with these attributes is in every case a story worth telling. Moreover, they represent the kind of power that can flicker from continent to continent in a nanosecond, borne along through the bowels of the computers that drive modern finance. What these people do, and say, and think, is important in Hong Kong. And in London, New York, Toronto and Sydney. If we live in a global economy, these are some of those who make the globe spin. More than that, they represent, in a direct and personal way, the links that will join – or not – the economies of the West to the mushrooming economy of China. They are very conscious, as you will hear in their own words, that they are on what the financial writers like to call the 'cutting edge' of the new economy, and equally conscious of the fact that the cutting edge is not a place to fall asleep. In short, what these people do is important in itself and, in a global sense, to all of us.

Finally, they are wonderful photographic portraits, are they not? We, the authors, need have no modesty on this score. Look on pages 158–9, where Frank Chao, owner of one of the largest container shipping lines on the surface of the globe, a man of presence and grávity, is hamming it up singing a karaoke version of 'Mona Lisa'. We were there, we saw it happen, we saw Lord Snowdon take the pictures, but we still don't know how it was done. There is something in the special vision of a world-class photographer which communicates itself to the subject, as well as to the audience.

The interviewer's job is difficult because language is precise, the subject sees the probe coming and quickly throws up elaborate verbal defences or evasions. Many of these people had been interviewed before, few had faced a photographer of the stature or talent of Snowdon. They could defend themselves in an interview by delivering answers by rote, Snowdon stripped them naked with subtle and distracting distress.

Many people wonder if Hong Kong will survive its return to mainland China rule. Will the rule of law apply, will the streets be safe for tourists and foreign businessmen and will Hong Kong continue to be a great international centre for business and finance? Most worry about the effect of mainland Chinese politics and bureaucracy on Hong Kong's business environment and population. They see mainland China pressing in on Hong Kong, stifling the confidence and ingenuity of its people.

Others suggest that Hong Kong has delivered an infusion of energy that will eventually transform China and her great cities into Hong Kong's image. Hong Kong has always served as a window on the West: but the flow of the current has been reversed, and energy, ideas and investment are pouring into China, not only from Hong Kong but from much of the rest of the world. They point out that internal reforms are pushing China towards the kind of free market environment that has allowed Hong Kong its tremendous success. They say the momentum is now too great to be stopped. China seems prepared to accept ideas as well as the hard currency investment it so desperately needs. If this is true then Hong Kong may be serving as a model for cities such as Shanghai, Guangzhou and Beijing.

But there are variables that render the picture of China more complex and disturbing. Who really leads this nation of 1.2 billion? That can't be answered easily today. What kind of leadership can we expect from the next generation of rulers? And what havoc might the struggle for power bring? The question of leadership is the most troubling for the Western observer and investor. And if the new leadership causes a crisis of confidence, what will happen to the billions of dollars flowing in to rebuild and modernize China? If that river of currency dries up and there are widespread bankruptcies and unemployment, China could find herself thrown back into darkness and isolation. This will probably be the determining factor in the future Hong Kong

9

may – or may not – look forward to after 1 July 1997. In an irony typical of our time, history seems to be serving up a mystery every bit as complex and profound as the expiration of a treaty is simple and clear.

We see Hong Kong's future tied inextricably to China's evolution; soon, it will cease to be a British colony and will become simply the most Westernized city in China. When the trappings of the colony disappear, what kind of Chinese city will remain? What will its place be in China?

Presently, one-third of China's trade with the rest of the world passes through Hong Kong. Hong Kong is the world's eighth biggest trading economy and boasts the largest container terminal in the world. In the ten years since the signing of the Joint Declaration, Hong Kong has maintained an average growth rate of 5.5 per cent. Much of this growth has been made possible by the opening up of the mainland, and the tremendous increase in cross-border trade and investment. Hong Kong's manufacturing sector has been able to remain competitive by moving inland, where cheap labour is plentiful. In the neighbouring province of Guangdong, Hong Kong investors have created over 30,000 enterprises employing approximately 3 million workers. Guangdong's industrial output has been the highest in China since the 1980s and posted a 36.5 per cent increase from 1992 to 1993.

Investments from Hong Kong account for 64 per cent of total foreign investment in China, exceeding US $13 billion, but investments from mainland China into Hong Kong are in excess of US $20 billion. This figure represents holdings by state-owned corporations in banking, transport, telecommunications, property development and real estate. Newly affluent citizens of Guangdong Province have even been known to purchase flats in Hong Kong with suitcases full of cash. This speaks as much for their wealth – as these are some of the most expensive flats per square foot in the world – as it does of their confidence in Hong Kong's status as a Special Administrative Region after 1997. Will Hong Kong develop into a kind of Monaco on the Mediterranean of the South China Sea, free of punitive taxes and disruptive politics?

Wealth first came to Hong Kong in the 1950s through manufacturing and shipping but because of ever-increasing labour costs the manufacturing sector is now shrinking and moving inland to the neighbouring Guangdong Province. Guangzhou (formerly Canton), a city of 6 million, resembles to those who knew it, the Hong Kong of the 1950s. Today, Hong Kong is making a very rapid transition from a manufacturing-based economy to a service-based economy.

In the 1980s, the investment firm Morgan Stanley had approximately 400 executives stationed in Tokyo and only 60 in Hong Kong. These numbers are now reversed, the numbers falling in Japan because of the recession, but rising in Hong Kong because of increased or anticipated business. Most of the world's largest banks and investment houses are moving into Hong Kong to exploit China's current or future, economic boom.

However, the cultural ground from which business in Hong Kong grows is of a very different texture from that in New York or London. Most people are struck by the polite and deferential manner of most of Hong Kong's citizens. But the more you ask of people, the more specific and demanding your request, the greater the distance that can grow between the two of you. Rarely will anyone actually say no. If you send a letter offering a service or asking a favour and receive no reply, then this means no. This makes no sense, and is hugely frustrating, to the Westerner accustomed to a direct response from a direct question. It also irks our sense of completion. We feel left hanging. But no answer means no. The Chinese believe that to say no, to reject your offer or enquiry, is to make you lose face, or be dishonoured. Some Hong Kong Chinese take advantage of this and remain equivocal only in order to keep their options open.

Any discussion of the 'Chineseness' of Hong Kong should recollect that one of the earliest conflicts between Britain and China arose because Britain's first emissary refused to genuflect before the Emperor. The emissary believed such action was humiliating to his person and office. But to the Chinese this was simply a gesture of respect to the Emperor, perceived no differently than a handshake between strangers, as the first step towards friendship and trust.

The Chinese invest tremendous significance in numbers. The billionaire Cheng Yu-tung, chairman of New World Development, is chauffeured around Hong Kong in a Rolls Royce bearing the licence-plate number 8888. Licence plates bearing such lucky numbers are regularly auctioned off by the government and raise millions of dollars for charities.

The Chinese can be terrifically superstitious, and incredibly sensitive to double meanings. The word for tiger in Cantonese has a similar sound to the word for hardship. A porcelain tiger would not be a wise wedding gift. The same is true for the sound of the Cantonese word for clock; not only does it sound similar to the word for attending a funeral, but it is also too much a reminder of the passage of time, or age and therefore death. Certainly not something to send as a gift. A wristwatch is something else; wristwatches of every make and in every price range are sold at every street corner. They are seen as sound and practical investments – particularly Rolexes – and eminently portable.

Feng shui experts are paid large fees for advice on the important aspects or events of life. The date and time for weddings or funerals, the location of the front door to a residence, or the arrangement of the tables and chairs in an office all require the *feng shui* expert's approval.

These are some of the more obvious Chinese characteristics. The actual sensibility of the Hong Kong Chinese is something one only experiences if one spends a period of time with an individual. It is dangerous and difficult to typify this experience as it varies with each person one encounters. But it is fair to say that one is always left a little unsure of the exact meaning of things. This is not necessarily bad, for it encourages the visitor to be clear and to listen carefully, which usually leads to greater understanding and respect.

Moreover, in Hong Kong you can never be sure who you may be talking to. In a curious way this makes it a most democratic society. In the West we quickly classify people by the car they drive or the clothes they wear. Billionaire Li Ka-shing is proud of his ten-year-old suits and $50 quartz watch. And Sally Aw Sian, the CEO of Sing Tao Newspapers and heiress to the Tiger Balm fortune, could be mistaken for the most casually dressed housewife. But their eyes reveal all. Both Li Ka-shing and Sally Aw Sian have eyes that miss nothing and reveal only a piercing intelligence. Li Ka-shing's eyes, when focused to respond to a troubling question, cut into you like razor blades.

This cultural duality, an ability to function in a Western environment – be more British than the British – but still see the world through Chinese eyes, speaks of the confidence brought by a cultural heritage that has survived separation from mainland China. But it is also one of the reasons the British have failed – even after all these years – to see the people of Hong Kong as being, above all else, Chinese. If it talks like an Englishman, if it dresses and even drives like an Englishman, then of course it must be an Englishman. Wrong! And the mounting anxiety in London over the fate of the people of Hong Kong after 1997, as expressed by the current Governor's awkward rush towards greater democratization, only makes sense if one sees the people of Hong Kong as British and Caucasian and not Chinese.

What is this indelible Chineseness beneath the surface and where does it come from? In large part it comes from the teachings of Confucius, which have dominated Chinese society for over two thousand years. It is a philosophy that is less concerned with what one may accomplish materially than with the development of the individual's moral character, and the search for 'Truth'. It is a philosophy whose influence has placed the scholar at the top of the pyramid of Chinese society. In ancient times, rigorous examinations were held to find the most brilliant scholars in the land. The most gifted were then joined in marriage to the daughters of the

11

Emperor. And though the merchant was placed at the bottom of society's pyramid, respect for learning is such that to this day many successful overseas Chinese, and most of Hong Kong's greatest entrepreneurs, sponsor schools and universities in mainland China. The focus is on an interior growth, a strength that cannot be measured by external or material manifestations. Integrity, honesty, the way of the mean and deference to others are all characteristics of Confucianism, and can be seen at work when Victor Li, eldest son of Li Ka-shing, says of his father, 'The most important thing I learned from him is how to be honourable and how to treat partners right.' Similarly, the younger son, Richard, says, 'If a ten per cent share is reasonable and you can get eleven per cent, take nine per cent, because then a hundred more deals will come to you.'

COMMERCE IN THE NINETEENTH CENTURY AND THE FOUNDING OF HONG KONG

By the early nineteenth century the British were finding it increasingly difficult to conduct trade with China through the port of Canton (Guangzhou). The bulk of their business was the selling of opium brought by boat from India. It was not only concern for the general health of its people that prompted China's government to declare opium illegal in 1799 and to launch an increasingly aggressive campaign to block its flow into the country, but also the threat to their balance of trade brought about by massive purchase of this highly addictive narcotic. The silver bullion that had been flowing into China for the purchase of silk, tea and porcelain was now flowing out at an alarming rate.

Foreigners could only reside in certain parts of Canton, they were not allowed to learn or speak Chinese, and they could only live in the city during the trading season, from October to March. These restrictions were largely ineffective in stemming the flow of opium, and after 1833, when the East India Company lost its monopoly over the manufacture and sale of the drug, foreign operators quickly multiplied the numbers involved in this astonishingly lucrative trade.

In March 1839 the Emperor Tao-Kuang appointed Lin Ze-xu (Lin Tse-hsu) to Canton as High Commissioner with specific orders to stamp out the opium trade. Lin wrote to Queen Victoria, who had just ascended to the British throne:

> *I am told that in your country opium smoking is forbidden under severe penalties. This means you are aware of how harmful it is . . . so long as you do not take it yourselves, but continue to make and tempt the people of China to buy it, you will be showing yourself careful of your own life, but careless of the lives of other people, indifferent in your greed for gain to the harm you do to others; such conduct is repugnant to human feelings and at variance with the Way of Heaven . . . I now give you my assurance that we mean to cut off this powerful drug for ever. What is here forbidden to consume, your dependencies must be forbidden to manufacture, and what has already been manufactured Your Majesty must immediately search out and throw to the bottom of the sea, and never again allow such a poison to exist . . . you will be showing that you understand the principles of Heaven . . . by respectful obedience to our commands.*

Neither moral argument nor seriousness of tone caused London to take action. Nor was Lin taken seriously closer to home, at least not by the foreign traders, even though he imprisoned thousands of Chinese, and had at least one a day executed for participating in the trade. Finally, Lin demanded that the foreign merchants hand over all of their opium. He surrounded their settlement in Canton with troops and cut off food and water. After a blockade of six weeks, Captain Charles Elliot, RN, the British government's representative as Chief Superintendent of Trade, authorized the surrender of 20,283 chests of opium.

The British withdrew down the Pearl River to Macao. When the Portuguese governor there expressed reluctance to becoming involved in a dispute with China, the British boarded their ships and sailed south to the sheltered harbour of Hong Kong. In his zeal, Lin called upon the Chinese of Kowloon and Hong Kong to cut off supplies to the British, intending to force their return to Canton and submission to the ban against opium, or to see them leave the territory entirely. Tensions continued to rise until the arrival of the twenty-eight-gun Royal Navy frigate HMS *Volage*. In response to a threat from the Chinese, Elliot ordered Captain Smith of the *Volage* to open fire on the men-of-war junks forming the blockade. The junks were no match for the Royal Navy guns, and the incident ended with the Chinese forces humiliated.

Lord Palmerston, the British Foreign Secretary, took advantage of the circumstances to argue for a commercial treaty with China to stabilize relations, or a permanent settlement for Sino-British commercial relations. An expeditionary force arrived from India in June 1840, beginning the First Opium War (1840–2).

The Emperor dismissed Lin and replaced him with a commissioner, who turned out to have a greater understanding of and respect for the strength of the British forces. Quishan (Keshen) dismantled the defence at Canton and promised the British a peaceful resumption of trade. But it was too little, too late. The British reacted with a successful military operation in January 1841 against the forts guarding the entrance to the Pearl River. Quishan had little alternative but to surrender to the British demands.

Under the convention of Cheuenpi (Chuanbi), 20 January 1841, $6 million would be offered as compensation for the opium Lin had confiscated and destroyed, trading could resume as before in Canton, and the island of Hong Kong, until then a barren, rocky, sparsely settled haven for river pirates, would be ceded to the British. But the agreement was never signed. Neither side was happy. Quishan was sentenced to death and then exiled, like Lin, to the wilds of Turkestan. The British were equally displeased with Captain Elliot who, they thought, had settled for far too little. He too was exiled and ended his career as British Consul-General in Texas. Despite official discontent, a naval party had raised the British flag at Possession Point on Hong Kong Island on 26 January 1841, marking the formal occupation of their new possession.

Elliot's successor, Sir Henry Pottinger, arrived in August 1841, determined to bring China to its knees, and pushed British forces inland to the gates of Nanking. The Chinese capitulated and the treaty of Nanking was signed on 29 August 1842, ending the war and formalizing the surrender of Hong Kong to the British. The crucial clause reads:

> *It being obviously necessary, and desirable, that British subjects should have some port whereat they may careen and refit their ships, when required, and keep Stores for that purpose, His Majesty the Emperor of China cedes to Her Majesty the Queen of Great Britain the Island of Hong Kong, to be possessed in perpetuity by Her Britannic Majesty, Her Heirs, and successors and to be governed by such laws and regulations as Her Majesty the Queen of Great Britain shall see fit to direct.*

The island thus ceded was tiny – barely twenty-nine miles, or seventy-five kilometres, square – but it turned out to have many natural harbours, the largest of which is Victoria Harbour, at the foot of Victoria Peak. (Her Majesty liked having things named after her; the city of Hong Kong's official name is Victoria, and there may even be some who call it that.) This beautiful, sheltered, deep-water port was to become one of the greatest trading centres in the world, and the Chinese might have been even more reluctant to part with it had they known that in 1842.

Distrust and conflict continued, and a second Anglo-Chinese war followed (1856–8), propelled by the attitude expressed by Lord Palmerston, who became Prime Minister of Britain in 1855, in the quotation at the top of this chapter.

13

Hostilities broke out after Chinese police in Canton boarded the *Arrow*, a British vessel, in search of pirates. The ship was owned by a Chinese, but was registered in Hong Kong and was under the command of a British captain. The Chinese denied that the *Arrow* was a foreign vessel and refused to apologize. Governor Bowring took advantage of the incident and ordered the Royal Navy to take the four forts guarding the approaches to Canton.

Palmerston sent the Earl of Elgin to Hong Kong in mid-1857, with instructions to demand compensation, the resumption of treaty rights, and the instalment of a British representative in Peking. Elgin captured Canton at the end of the year and continued further north, taking the Taku forts in May 1858. He occupied Tiensin (Tianjin) and negotiated a treaty ending hostilities, and finally giving the British the right of diplomatic representation in China. But the first British envoy, Sir Frederick Bruce, who had been the first Colonial Secretary in Hong Kong, was fired on at Taku (Dagu) Bar on his way to Peking to present his credentials. Elgin returned with an even greater force and upon reaching Shanghai issued an ultimatum which the Chinese rejected.

The Taipings, a revolutionary army of more than one million, organized by a poor school teacher, Hung Hsiu-chuan, had been fighting the Ching rulers and had occupied large parts of China. The Ching rulers saw the Taipings as a greater threat than the British, and decided to come to terms with the latter, hoping for help. Elgin entered Peking on 24 October and the Convention of Peking was signed, finally ratifying the Treaty of Tiensin. An additional clause was added to the Convention of Peking that had not been in the Treaty of Tiensin; this added the tip of Kowloon Peninsula, across from the island of Hong Kong, whose occupation provided greater security against mainland forces and additional sea front for godowns and barracks.

The defeat of China by the Japanese in the war of 1894–5 encouraged other nations to seek portions of China's territory. This made Britain anxious to preserve its already well-established settlement by seeking additional lands. Discussions between China and Britain began on 2 April 1898. China was prepared to lease additional land, but not to cede it. In early June 1898, the Convention of Peking was signed, granting Britain a further 365.5 square miles of territory. The 'New Territories' comprised the area north of Kowloon up to the Shum Chun (Shenzhen) River and included 235 tiny islands. The lease was to begin in July 1898 and will end on 30 June 1997.

HONG KONG IN THE TWENTIETH CENTURY

There are events in the life of a country, just as in the life of the individual, that shape character and colour destiny. The most striking moments in the history of any country occur when the whole population seems for a brief moment to come together as one. War, revolution or shared grief over the loss of a beloved national hero are the most obvious examples. In 1925, there were approximately 4,500 British citizens in Hong Kong, surrounded by some 725,000 Chinese. In that year, the Chinese majority found cause to unite for a general strike. The strength of their political will and the power of their numbers momentarily terrified the British authorities. Sir Reginald Stubbs, the Governor, harrumphed, 'Those who disturb the peace of the colony, will be treated, as is the way with the English, justly but sternly.'

The forces of Dr Sun Yat Sen had overthrown the Manchu dynasty in 1911, but because of China's vast size and many internal conflicts, a clear republic with Sun Yat Sen as President was never fully realized. The years leading up to Sun Yat Sen's death in 1925 were years of political infighting and turmoil, which provided a fertile ground for the birth of the Chinese Communist Party under the leadership of Mao Tse Tung.

The population of Hong Kong continued to be fed by refugees from this ongoing revolution. Those choosing Hong Kong as a refuge were attracted to the peace and stability of a British-ruled colony. But the myth of the British Empire was beginning to fade, and Britain's colonial rule had already been challenged by the Indian Mutiny. What could possibly provoke a population of refugees to rise up against their protectors? A population thriving under the British flag? It was simply a people recognizing that they had no choice in deciding the conditions under which they lived and the direction of their future. In fact, some of the very same reasons for which they had fled mainland China.

There had been minor riots about food prices in 1911 and a seaman's strike in 1922, but not until 1925 did the whole Chinese population of Hong Kong unite as one. External elements helped push the divisions within the community together. The death of Sun Yat Sen and anti-foreign riots in Shanghai inspired pride in the Chinese population, reminding them of their history, and inflaming resentment over foreign domination.

And what was this general strike about? What were the people's exorbitant demands? They wanted an eight-hour day, prohibition of child labour, an end to police brutality and segregation on the Peak (the upper levels of Victoria Peak, where only whites were allowed to live), a twenty-five per cent reduction in rents and labour representation on the Executive Council. The headline in *The South China Morning Post* read: LABOURERS' EXTRAORDINARY ATTITUDE.

This was a broad-based general strike supported by everyone from rickshaw men, hotel staff, bus and tram drivers and domestic workers. There was some violence, much talk of violence, and angry threats from all sides. There were runs on banks, land prices fell, and every day there were as many as twenty bankruptcies. However, very little changed until Hong Kong was attacked by Japanese forces on 8 December 1941. Pearl Harbor, the Philippines and Malaya were attacked at the same time, as part of the overall Japanese strategy to capture and control East and Southeast Asia.

The Japanese had seized Manchuria in 1932 and by 1937 had taken Beijing. Their invasion of China managed to stop the civil war and briefly unify the Kuomintang and the Communists under the command of Chiang Kai-shek. But by the autumn of 1939, the Japanese were as far south as Guangzhou (Canton) and had stationed troops along the frontier with Hong Kong. The British military could not agree as to how Hong Kong should be defended in the event of a Japanese attack, or if it should be defended at all. The island's defences were minimal, because the British saw Singapore as being more important strategically. Most, including the general population, assumed the Japanese would never bother attacking. The colony had business links with Japan and boasted a sizeable Japanese community. Nevertheless, preparations were made. British males were liable to conscription and, in June 1940, European women and children were evacuated to Australia.

The Japanese occupation of Indochina in 1941 was followed by American and British embargoes on all exports of steel and oil to Japan. Tensions in the Pacific increased. Minefields were laid and seventy-two pillboxes were constructed on Hong Kong Island.

On 8 December, the Japanese crossed the Chinese frontier into the New Territories. It took only four days for them to take control of the whole peninsula. The British defenders watched from Hong Kong Island as the Japanese forces massed on the Kowloon waterfront. Winston Churchill sent a message to the Governor, to tell him that 'there must be no thought of surrender', and the military experts believed that Hong Kong Island could hold out for at least four months, but it fell in little more than a week. Had the island's defences been greater, and the combined forces better trained and co-ordinated, the outcome would probably have been the same. This was the first organized armed conflict between the British and the Japanese. The greatest flaw in the British defences was their underestimation of Japanese will and their continuing belief in British racial superiority. The defeat was a rude and humiliating shock. Christmas Day 1941 marked the first time a British Crown Colony had ever surrendered to an enemy. The British lost approximately 2,000 with 1,300 seriously wounded; at least 4,000

15

civilians were killed, almost all Chinese; and 9,000 British, Indian and Canadian soldiers were taken prisoner. Canadians remain bitter that British arrogance trapped soldiers from two Canadian regiments in Hong Kong. They were sent in in November, and ordered to surrender one month later. Of 1,975 Canadians who surrendered, 557 never returned. The others spent four years in appalling conditions in prison camps.

For the people of Hong Kong, the Japanese occupation was simply the replacement of one imperial power with another, and more brutal one. Occupation was the greatest single test Hong Kong and its citizens had suffered. In March 1941, there were 1.4 million residents, several hundred thousand of whom were recently arrived refugees from the Japanese occupation of the mainland. At the time of the Japanese surrender in August 1945, the population had shrunk to 600,000.

In February 1945, US President Franklin D. Roosevelt suggested to the Soviets at Yalta that the British might be persuaded to surrender Hong Kong to the Nationalist forces under Chiang Kai-shek. This was an attempt to win Soviet support for his plans in the Pacific, and to appease China. Churchill was furious with the idea and the fact that the proposal had been made behind his back.

The British flag was raised on 18 August 1945 and Colonial Secretary Franklin Gimson was quickly sworn in as acting Governor by Chief Justice Sir Athol MacGregor on 29 August. The formal surrender came on 16 September, by which time the Nationalists and Communists had resumed their bitter war over control of China.

Anxiety increased in the colony when Mao declared the creation of the People's Republic of China from Tiananmen Gate on 1 October 1949. There was fear that the Communist forces might cross the border as easily as many refugees were doing daily. The Communists didn't take it back because they found themselves almost immediately facing the problem of Taiwan (occupied by Chiang Kai-shek and the Nationalist forces) and the Korean War, which had started within months of the establishment of the People's Republic of China. They wanted to be left alone to build this new kind of society, but at the same time they didn't want total isolation. So Hong Kong was left as their window on the world. They felt the British were of little threat, and that one day Hong Kong could be of real benefit. At the same time, they would make use of Hong Kong in banking, foreign exchange, trading and shipping. This is the pattern the optimists hope will be repeated in 1997.

These were the bloodiest years of the revolution and the flood of refugees into Hong Kong was tremendous. The 600,000 population of 1945 swelled to almost two million when the Communists sealed the border in 1950. This growth inspired astonishing resourcefulness. Coal was brought in from Indochina, rice and vegetables from Guangzhou, wood from Borneo, cotton from India and building supplies from Australia. The speed of the recovery surprised everyone, and by 1956 trade was half of pre-war levels in volume and more than double in dollar value. Many of the commercial banks, including the Hongkong Bank, were instrumental in the rebirth of industry and commerce. They were prepared to make advances for capital equipment and raw materials with no security except the strength of their personal relationship with factory owners. This established the loyalty and trust of the new industrialists whose business would eventually help make the Hongkong Bank one of the world's largest and most respected commercial banks.

DENG XIAOPING COMES TO POWER IN CHINA, 1978

The last two decades of Mao's life were China's twenty lost years. Tens of millions lost their lives from political purges, or famine brought about by mismanagement. The Great Leap Forward (1958–60) and the Cultural Revolution (1966–76) were initiated by Mao to continue – or to re-invigorate – the ideological reform of China. But they were based on ideas and abstractions, and seemed aimed more at the removal of opposition, real or imagined, than at solving real problems.

The Cultural Revolution sent Deng into exile in 1969. Mao's health began to fail in the early 1970s, and the Gang of Four, led by Jiang Qing, Mao's actress wife, began a reach for power through their control of the propaganda department of the Communist Party. Zhou Enlai, who seemed the rightful heir to Mao, was diagnosed with terminal liver cancer in 1973. Zhou had always tried to be a moderating influence on Mao's excesses. He had remained loyal and continued to have Mao's confidence. But when it became clear that he might not outlive Mao he began an effort to ensure the succession of a leader in line with the direction he felt China had to undertake to rebuild herself. Zhou orchestrated Deng's rehabilitation and return to Beijing and a position of authority in 1973. In 1975, Zhou delivered his speech outlining the programme for his Four Modernizations in an effort to focus energy and attention on the restructuring and modernization of industry, agriculture, science/technology and defence. He would not live long enough to direct this new movement, but the principles he outlined would become the first order of business for Deng when he finally assumed power in 1978.

Upon his return to Beijing, Deng faced the task of overcoming the terrible cost of the Cultural Revolution. He began a complete reorganization of the People's Liberation Army in the summer of 1975, and worked hard rehabilitating members of the Party who had been out of favour and whose managerial skills were now so desperately needed for the overhaul of essential industries. In spite of Zhou's failing health, he worked together with Deng to try to pull China's agriculture and industry into the twentieth century. But there was much intrigue, and a paranoid and feeble Mao could be easily influenced to turn against even such trusted colleagues as Zhou and Deng.

Swayed by the scheming Jiang Qing, Mao launched a formal campaign of criticism against Deng in November 1975. Zhou Enlai's physical condition was deteriorating rapidly. It seemed as if Jiang Qing and the Gang of Four had won the struggle for power. Zhou Enlai died in January 1976. Deng delivered a eulogy at the funeral praising Zhou's life and work. It was the last time Deng would appear in public until after Mao's death.

Deng had been able to accomplish a great deal in a very short period of time – in large part because of support from the military and the esteem with which he was regarded by members of the Party. In 1975, he had increased the output of agriculture by 15.1 per cent and industry by 4.6 per cent. The gross output of both in 1974 had only been 1 per cent over the previous year. The foundation for China's economic boom of the 1980s and 1990s had been laid. Deng had showed China its potential. Then, politics and intrigue – once again – brought positive reforms, and forward movement, to a halt.

Rather than giving more authority to the Gang of Four after Deng's ouster, Mao promoted the little-known Hua Guofeng to the position of acting Premier. This seemed to incite the Gang to publish outrageous denunciations of both Zhou Enlai and Deng. In the past, such propaganda would have surely destroyed the reputations, if not the lives, of its victims. The public might have accepted attacks against Deng, but genuine affection for the recently deceased Zhou caused a public outpouring of sentiment for Zhou, and open demonstrations of anger towards the Gang.

Politburo members began paying last respects to the comatose Mao in August 1976. Deng was in hiding in Canton under the protection of the commandant of the Canton military, General Xu Shiyou, and the Governor of Guangdong Province, Wei Guoqing. Mao's death seemed likely to signal the outbreak of open warfare between those loyal to Deng and the Shanghai based forces of the Gang of Four.

Mao Tse Tung died on 9 September 1976. Marshal Ye Jianying, the powerful military commander supporting Deng, heard that the Gang was preparing a coup for 7, 8 or 9 October. The Standing Committee of the Politburo was brought together on the evening of 6 October under the pretext of approving the proofs of volume five of Mao's selected writings. Two of the Gang of Four were members of the Standing Committee, the third member was given a special invitation to attend. The three members of the Gang arrived at the hall separately. When they entered, Hua Guofeng, acting Premier, rose and read out an indictment against them prepared by the Politburo. They were led away under arrest. Jiang Qing was arrested later that evening.

Deng did not immediately take control, or even assume the high posts that had been stripped from him in spring 1976. Hua Guofeng had been instrumental in bringing down the Gang of Four and was not about to give up power easily. It was not until August 1977, after the Eleventh Party Congress, that it became clear that Deng Xiaoping, with the backing of Marshal Ye Jianying, had finally outmanoeuvred Hua for control. Deng spent the next year consolidating his support within the Party and working for the rehabilitation of the managers and trained professionals still suffering exile or imprisonment as a result of the purges of the Cultural Revolution.

In December 1978, at the Third Plenary of the Eleventh Central Committee, Deng finally laid out his programmes for reform and opening up to the West. Deng also began to bring a younger generation into positions of authority. He sent Zhao Ziyang to Sichuan Province, which had suffered nine years of famine, and Wan Li to Anhui, also a province suffering from years of famine and poverty. Here began the economic reforms that would soon spread throughout China. Wan Li eliminated Mao's communal system. He allowed each family their own plot of land and a share in the profits their crops might bring. The peasant owners negotiated a contract to sell their grain to the State, and whatever they produced in excess of what had been committed to the State could be sold on the open market for whatever it might bring. By the end of the first season, the peasants had produced enough to feed themselves, fulfil their obligations to the State contract, and have a surplus to sell on the open market. By the time the Party officially approved the system in 1982, it had spread throughout the country. The past fifteen years have seen these principles applied to many aspects of China's economy, resulting in its current economic boom.

Why discuss Deng's rise to power when our subject is Hong Kong? Because it is important to understand how difficult his rise to power was, how tenuous the hold on power in China is, and how much is at stake when power is transferred to the next generation of rulers. Little seems to have changed within the governing body to suggest that the transition will be smooth, and that the direction the country has been taking over the past fifteen years will continue unchanged. This is China – a very different master than parliamentary Britain.

THE HONG KONG BOUNCE

My father, Sir Elly Kadoorie, used to say that Hong Kong was like a hard rubber ball, the harder you threw it down, the higher it bounced back.
Lord Kadoorie

SINO–BRITISH JOINT DECLARATION ON HONG KONG, 1984

Lord Kadoorie of China Light & Power, asked about the dangers to business of the coming transfer of sovereignty replied, 'My father, Sir Elly Kadoorie, used to say that Hong Kong was like a hard rubber ball, the harder you threw it down, the higher it bounced back.' Many of the entrepreneurs we spoke to shrugged their shoulders at the question and reminded us of the many times Hong Kong had been written off. They'd seen it all before: bank runs, stock market collapse, riots in the streets, and the flight of capital and skilled professionals. They'd survived it then, and would again.

But the picture has changed. In the past, China seemed indifferent to the confidence the international community showed in Hong Kong. Hong Kong was Britain's responsibility, and capitalist. Today, however, China's economic boom is being fuelled from this spout and any threat to the flow of capital feeding the new economy is a threat to the stability of the whole nation. It is therefore in China's interest to ensure a reasonable and peaceful transfer of sovereignty. The Sino-British Joint Declaration on the question of Hong Kong (1984) sets out the terms of return in this spirit. And the Basic Law of the Hong Kong Special Administrative Region of the People's Republic of China (1990) can be seen as an effort to assure the international community that the laws and customs essential to Hong Kong's past success will remain in place after 1 July 1997. They are both efforts to preserve business confidence in Hong Kong, and speak of how important Hong Kong has become in China's blueprint for the future.

Confidence is about emotion, and emotions are affected by more than can be covered by these two documents. Will the Hong Kong of the People's Republic of China have the resilience to bounce back like the rubber ball of earlier times? It's very difficult to say. But separation from British control, and attachment to China's fate, changes the material nature of Sir Elly's rubber ball for ever.

Hong Kong Island was ceded to Great Britain in perpetuity with the signing of The Treaty of Nanking in 1842. But the New Territories, the land just north of the Kowloon Peninsula up to the Shenzhen River, was only leased from China in the Convention of Peking in 1898. Britain has no option but to return the New Territories at the expiration of the treaty. But what of Hong Kong Island and the tip of the Kowloon Peninsula? They were ceded in perpetuity. Legally, Britain has the right to deal with them as it pleases. There seem to be three possible options. Hold on to Hong Kong but be prepared to supply them should the Chinese cut off water, power and air access. The logistics of this nightmare would make the Berlin Airlift look like meals on wheels for shut-ins! Not a practical option. What about giving Hong Kong independence? A Rhodesia of the East? China would never allow it. The only practical solution, then, was to begin negotiations with mainland China over the return of Hong Kong Island at the time of the expiration of the lease on the New Territories, 1 July 1997.

Pressure to begin discussions began in the late 1970s with Deng's outward-looking reforms. Most of China's foreign exchange came from selling food and water to Hong Kong. It was not difficult or disruptive to expand these routes into international linkages for investment and expertise to enter China. By 1980, China had begun to set up Special Economic Zones as a means of containing the spiritual and ideological pollution that contact with the capitalist world would surely bring. The first Special Economic Zone was established around the city of Shenzhen, just across the border from the New Territories. It was also hoped that these special zones would draw foreign investment as they were separated – however cosmetically – from the strict Communist ideology of the rest of China.

Beijing came up with the concept of Special Administrative Regions in 1982. The idea was to accommodate the return of territory functioning under different economic and judicial systems. China was looking beyond Hong Kong, to the return of Macao in 1999, and the eventual re-unification of Taiwan. The fact that Beijing had accommodated Hong Kong's very different economic and judicial systems with its programme of Special Administrative Regions seemed to assure the international community of Hong Kong's viability after 1 July 1997. In July 1983, Britain and China began fourteen months of formal talks to work out the details of the transfer of sovereignty.

Britain's Prime Minister, Margaret Thatcher, argued for the involvement of the people of Hong Kong in the negotiations. She described the situation in terms of a three-legged stool (China, Britain and Hong Kong); if one leg is removed, the stool becomes unstable. But to call for the people of Hong Kong to play an equal role would require more real democracy in the

19

colony. Britain could hardly argue for an equal role for Hong Kong if the territory's top government officials were British expatriates appointed by the British Foreign Office. When the Governor of Hong Kong, Sir Edward Youde, joined the British negotiators he was asked exactly who he represented. He said, 'I am the Governor of Hong Kong . . . I represent the people of Hong Kong.' But how could he represent the people of Hong Kong when he had been appointed by the British government? It would be more appropriate to say that the Governor represents the interests of Great Britain, and governs the people of Hong Kong. The British were only fooling themselves. (This point is important to remember when examining the actions and policy of the present Governor, Chris Patten.)

The only card the British had to play during the negotiations seemed to be the value of a prosperous Hong Kong. Beijing was only interested in negotiating the terms and conditions of return. The longer the talks went on, the more international confidence in Hong Kong's future fell. The British card was quickly losing whatever value it may have had. The British finally relented, and accepted discussions focused on the specifics of the handover. It was at this point that the Chinese stated that Hong Kong's present social system could continue for fifty years after 1997, and discussions began on the structure of the Basic Law.

In early 1984, Jardine Matheson, the oldest trading company in the colony, announced its plans to move its holding company to Bermuda. Deng Xiaoping then announced that troops of the People's Liberation Army would be stationed in Hong Kong after 1997. These declarations shook the confidence of the business community, and woke Hong Kong's citizens to the realities ahead. Prominent Executive Council members travelled to London and Beijing in an effort to play a role in the negotiations. They were not able to persuade either side to include them in the negotiations, nor were they shown much respect. The experience did, however, inspire the beginnings of a multi-party democracy movement in Hong Kong that continues to this day.

One of the most contentious issues discussed during the negotiations was the question of nationality. At the time of the talks in 1984, there were approximately 2.8 million people who were British Dependent Territories citizens. These people used British documents for travel but had no right of abode in Great Britain. After much discussion, and with considerable reticence, China finally agreed to allow the use of British Dependent Territories documents only for international travel after 1997. The documents would not be valid for travel in Hong Kong or China, could only be held by those born before 1 July 1997, and could not be passed to future generations.

The Sino-British Joint Declaration on the Question of Hong Kong was signed by Margaret Thatcher and Zhao Ziyang, the Chinese Prime Minister, on 19 December 1984. The Basic Law of the Hong Kong Special Administrative Region of The People's Republic of China was passed in Beijing in 1990 and is the companion document outlining the laws, and the administration of law, in Hong Kong after 1 July 1997.

TIANANMEN SQUARE, 1989

The most striking of Deng Xiaoping's reforms of the late 1970s was perhaps Democracy Wall, approximately 600 feet of wall space not far from Tiananmen Square. Written dissent, slogans and criticism soon covered the wall. It was an effort to allow students and others to let off some steam. Deng had the wall scrubbed clean before the end of 1979 as it was attracting a great deal of international attention and encouraging greater and greater dissent.

A series of student demonstrations in 1986 and 1987 alarmed the Party leaders. The students had picked up the ideas of democracy and freedom, and seemed to be offering them up as a serious alternative to Communist rule. Deng removed Hu Yaobang, Secretary General of the Party in January 1987. Hu had come to be seen as the member of the government whose ideology most resembled the forward-looking student movement. An official campaign was launched against 'bourgeois liberalization'. But the danger died away from its own lack of momentum before the campaign could identify and consume any real victims. The interlude was brief. Dissent became a concern again in the spring of 1988.

Inflation accompanied Deng's reforms. The rise in price of such basic goods as gasoline, oil, seed and pesticide caused widespread discontent. A conflict was brewing between the hardliners, who wanted to slow Deng's reforms, and Deng and Party Secretary Zhao Ziyang, who felt these problems a necessary evil that would eventually be overcome by market forces. But the Party stood against them, and in the spring of 1988 the economy was taken from Deng and Zhao and put in the hands of Premier Li Peng.

Tension over economic problems, and the struggle for control of the direction of the Party, carried into early spring 1989. Hu Yaobang, who had been removed from his post for bourgeois sympathies, died on 15 April. His death injected life into the dormant student movement; he became their martyr. The students connected Hu's death with the Party's suppression of his – and therefore their – ideas. The Party did not act decisively, probably because of the distraction caused by the internal struggle for power. By 20 April, the students occupied Tiananmen Square. The government had two choices: remove the students by force or negotiate.

Mikhail Gorbachev was scheduled to visit Beijing on 15 May. The hardliners, backing Li Peng, argued for a forceful and harsh resolution. Zhao Ziyang spoke for moderation. All the while, the international press was pouring into Beijing to cover the Deng/Gorbachev talks, and sending out to the rest of the world scenes of mass demonstrations. It appeared that Deng had lost control of the country. He was certainly humiliated. He would have to do something dramatic to regain face and the confidence of the Party.

The last opportunity for resolution probably occurred when Zhao Ziyang visited the hunger-striking students on 19 May. He was conciliatory and understanding. Li Peng also came to Tiananmen on the 19th, but more out of some concern for what the emotional Zhao might do or say. The students sensed the split in the government and the fact that Zhao's forces were fast losing power. They called off the hunger strike that evening, although the occupation of Tiananman Square continued. If the government had not been divided, it probably could have taken action to end the demonstration at that time.

The moment passed. Deng declared marshal law. This inflamed the students and the demonstration seemed to regain momentum. Word spread of troops moving towards Beijing. But once again tensions began to ease, and the students seemed ready to disband. A vote was held and 220 schools wanted to end the demonstration, against 160 prepared to stay. The student leaders searched for a means to keep the demonstration going. Students of the Central Academy of Fine Arts, not far from Tiananmen Square, were asked to construct a sculpture of the Chinese Goddess of Democracy. The figure they constructed bore a striking resemblance to the American Statue of Liberty. The 37-foot-high sculpture energized the demonstrators. International media loved it. But still the numbers in the square were falling, and the demonstration dying.

The decision to clear Tiananmen Square was taken by Deng on Friday, 2 June. The Twenty-seventh and Thirty-eighth armies would do the job, supplemented by units from each of China's military districts. The bloodletting would be a shared experience, so as to seem the will of the whole nation.

Columns of armoured vehicles began to pour into Beijing. As they moved towards Tiananmen Square, crowds of students and passers-by ran out in front of the tanks. They could not imagine the tanks not stopping. But the decision had been made to end the demonstrations

21

with a show of force. The tanks left the streets littered with crushed bodies. The students in Tiananmen Square could hear the tanks and troops approaching. Word had also spread of the slaughter. The few thousand remaining in the square expected little mercy. The troops had been instructed to keep the violence out of view of the international media. Camera crews were assaulted and cameras and videos confiscated.

One of the first targets was the Goddess of Democracy, which was knocked to the pavement and crushed. As the sun began to rise on the morning of 4 June, the remaining students surrendered and were marched out of the square under the eyes of the soldiers of the People's Liberation Army. Some witnesses claim mass execution followed the students' surrender. It is certain that some of these students were never seen again. They were either executed, imprisoned, or they fled. Initially the government claimed few casualties. Witnesses at the scene estimate 3–400 demonstrators killed in the square with another 1–2,000 killed in Beijing.

On 9 June, Deng and Yang Shangkun appeared in public to congratulate the People's Liberation Army for the courage they showed in putting down the insurrection. Medals were commissioned to commemorate the action. The hardliners had prevailed. Deng had held onto power – barely. Zhao Ziyang became the scapegoat. Some argued that he was responsible for the demonstrations and should be put on trial. But Zhao had been Deng's protégé, and in large part had only been following Deng's direction; to put Zhao on trial would be to put Deng on trial, too.

Jiang Zemin replaced Zhao Ziyang as Party Secretary. Jiang Zemin and Li Peng were the chief beneficiaries of the Tiananmen massacre. Their rise within the Party has continued. Today, they hold the posts of Premier (Li Peng) and President (Jiang Zemin), the most powerful government positions in China.

The indecisiveness of the government in dealing with the students prior to 4 June, and the massacre itself, speak of a government out of touch with its people, a government losing its mandate to rule. If Deng had been ousted in 1989, and one of the younger generation had taken control of the government, the question of succession, and concern over the direction China will take after 1997, would have been answered. In many respects little has changed since 1989. The hardliners have the upper hand, and the economic problems of Deng's modernist reforms are worse, not better. What will happen during the inevitable succession struggle? How long will it take? Years?

The hardliners seem placed to take control. We have seen their lack of tolerance for social unrest, and their readiness to use the military against unarmed civilians. What will bring pressure to bear on the system first? Dissatisfaction with the succession or social unrest from unemployment, inflation and corruption? It seems less a question of what, than when.

THE LAST GOVERNOR

The world was shocked by the brutality of the Tiananmen massacre. Hong Kong was stunned. Tens of thousands paraded through the streets wearing black armbands. The stock market fell twenty-five per cent. The people of Hong Kong were united in their shock and disgust at what the Chinese government had done to its own people, and filled with fear at what this might mean for life in Hong Kong after 1997. How could Britain possibly hand them over to such a brutal regime?

There was pressure on Britain to renegotiate the Joint Declaration, and to allow Hong Kong Chinese the right of abode in Britain. Margaret Thatcher refused to consider right of abode to those holding Hong Kong British passports. The only options Britain considered reasonable were to press Beijing for further assurance that Hong Kong's way of life would remain unchanged for fifty years, and to tell the people of Hong Kong that they would introduce more democracy into Hong Kong's system of government. But surely one would cancel out the other? Democracy would close the door on discussions with Beijing, and assurance of Hong Kong's special status after 1997 would only be offered by Beijing if the status quo remained unchanged. A no-win situation or a stage for political theatre? And would the spectacle be a drama, a comedy, a horror show or a tragedy?

The retirement of David Wilson as Governor of Hong Kong was announced in January 1992. Chris Patten was named as his successor, and Hong Kong's last Governor. Most of Hong Kong's Governors came from the diplomatic corps, many spoke Chinese and were referred to as 'China hands' because of their experience and knowledge of the East. Chris Patten is a politician. He was the elected Member of Parliament for Bath and Chairman of the Conservative Party. He has been combative and confrontational from the beginning. Almost immediately, he initiated reforms that would introduce greater democracy into Hong Kong's system of government. He claims that these reforms do not violate the spirit or the letter of the Joint Declaration or the Basic Law. But Patten's actions seem hollow gestures. Surely Beijing will wipe the slate clean on 1 July 1997, and re-interpret the agreements as they see fit. Why is this Governor causing a fuss? Why not do everything possible to ensure a smooth and honourable transfer? Why threaten the prosperity of Hong Kong – which is, after all, its only resource? His motives may spring from 1989 and Thatcher's belief that greater democracy in the colony would show the people of Hong Kong how to stand up to their new masters. Surely too little, too late. And if democracy is so important a right, why has Britain waited 150 years before introducing it?

Cynics claim Patten is playing to the Western audience. His tilting at windmills seems romantic and heroic from afar, something he will use to fuel his future political career in England. But Patten is not a stupid man, and should not be underestimated. Certainly it is too little, too late; but it's also better late than never. The people of Hong Kong have been discouraged from organized politics more from comfort and complacency than because of British policy. The only time they expressed a uniform political will was during the general strike of 1925. Perhaps Patten wants to wake the sleeping giant. Perhaps nothing would make him happier than to have the population rise up against him, insisting he cease and desist. Whatever the motives, why not make them clearer? Can all the distress and insecurity be blamed on inadequate or incompetent public relations? At this point the underlying fear for the peoples of Hong Kong must be the effect of Patten's actions on China, and the price they might have to pay for them after the takeover.

It is through an examination of the history of the cultures of Britain and China that we can best understand how Hong Kong has reached this point in time, but it is through an analysis of the nature of the population and the character of the people that we may just be able to glimpse the path Hong Kong will take in these final years leading up to 1 July 1997.

What might happen when these disciplined and resourceful people truly come to realize the full implications of their return to mainland China? When there is nowhere to run, no more passports to be had, when the divorce is final and they are to be turned over to a parent they barely know and have always feared? It's possible nothing will happen. It's possible people will say in the future that this was simply the paranoia produced when a Western point of view is superimposed on an Eastern culture. We've been wrong before. It's also possible that this present generation of Hong Kong citizens – with fifty per cent of the population now having been born and raised in Hong Kong – may just find its political voice. If the people of Hong Kong apply the same energy, and resolve to make that voice heard, as they have in creating one of the economic miracles of the late twentieth century, then it might become a mighty roar indeed. History tells us that anything can happen and nothing is impossible.

SPHERES OF INFLUENCE

MY FRIEND GEOFFREY HOWE ONCE COMPARED
HONG KONG TO A PRICELESS MING VASE. I HAVE TO SAY THAT
I DO NOT FIND THIS IMAGE APPROPRIATE. HONG KONG IS ACTUALLY
AS TOUGH AS OLD BOOTS. IT HAS NEEDED TO BE AS IT HAS FACED
CHALLENGES THROUGHOUT ITS HISTORY WHICH WOULD HAVE
SWAMPED LESS RESILIENT COMMUNITIES.

Baroness Dunn

When Chris Patten, the appointed British Governor of Hong Kong, leaves the colony, he is chauffeured out to the airport in a Bentley limousine bearing a licence plate that is a stylized representation of the British crown. Patten rejected the traditional, gold-braided Governor's habit and plumed hat when he took over his post in July 1992, but other trappings of the old regime remain, including the red and gold diadem on his licence. As his plane takes off, the chauffeur pulls out a screwdriver and unfastens the plate. Then he walks across and screws it onto the front bumper of the car parked next to it, the black Jaguar belonging to Patten's deputy, and Hong Kong's Chief Secretary, Anson Chan, the handsome woman whose portrait appears on page 33. Her plate, with the initials 'CS', goes into the boot.

When Patten returns, the licence plate is restored to the Bentley. Whether the power it represents flows back completely is a matter for conjecture. Patten and his plate are symbols of a fading empire, facing eclipse; Chan embodies the future. She is Chinese, born in Shanghai in 1940; and when the Governor flies out for the last time in 1997, she will still be here, while the symbolic plate will go into storage in some museum. She is one of the officials who are said to be

25

The wise man is not confused, the benevolent free of anxiety, and the bold has no fear.

on the 'through train' here; those whose power is expected to survive the shock of transition. She is involved in a balancing act between two regimes, and, so far, she is holding up well.

In this chapter, we are going to look at four individuals, beginning with Chan, who represent bureaucratic, business and political power, alone or in combination, and who together represent the senior spheres of influence in Hong Kong.

First, we will briefly examine the way the place works, in theory; then we will look at the Governor, and how he handles his job, and then we will meet practitioners of power who will not be flying back to Whitehall when the calendar turns to 1997. We will discover that Hong Kong is at once a thriving city and a small village; here, the parish pump may be on the fortieth floor of a smart office building, but the same rules apply. News travels faster than the speed of light, reputation is all, and gossip – or, if you prefer, the exchange of information – is the currency of decision-making, which circulates across the circles of power that bind these men and women together.

GUANXI, AND HOW IT WORKS

Hong Kong exists because of business. Conflicts arising out of the opium trade in the nineteenth century led to the colony's founding, and the river of investment directed through Hong Kong to feed China's modernization ensures its immediate future. In the past it was said that Hong Kong was run by the Jockey Club, the Chairman of the Hongkong and Shanghai Bank and the Governor – in that order. The interconnected spheres of influence of today are the Stock Exchange, an eclectic mix of individuals of power and influence, and the Governor. Why does the Governor rank third? In the past the Governor kept a low profile, and the administration did its best to balance business interests with the needs of the general population. Today's Governor is ferociously high profile, but the administration seems to be going along as before.

In a community devoted to commerce, it is not surprising that the Chairman of the Hongkong and Shanghai Bank would have held second place. He was sandwiched between the Jockey Club, which earned its authority by being run by a pool of the most influential expatriates in the colony, and the Governor, whose authority was granted by London and whose tenure was limited.

As Hong Kong progressed, and as local fortunes grew, Chinese banks began to compete with the Hongkong and Shanghai. By the mid-1960s, before an unfortunate and mysterious run on deposits, the Hang Seng Bank threatened to supersede the Hongkong and Shanghai Bank. But the development that changed the traditional spheres of influence was the listing on the Stock Exchange in the early 1970s of many of the big Hong Kong family-owned corporations. These were the development companies founded by men like Li Ka-shing, Cheng Yu-tung and Tak-sing Kwok.

The Jockey Club had been the centre of a traditional English old boys' network. The club of clubs. All the members of society who counted – primarily the British taipans – sat on its board, acted as its stewards and decided how the huge profits that gambling generated would be dispersed for the betterment of the general society. The stock market has replaced the morally superior attitude of the old boys' network with the practical power of raw wealth. The Hong Kong Stock Exchange is ranked sixth in the world in market capitalization, but it is still small enough that when it fell with the rest of the world's markets in 1987, the major families were able to inject life and confidence back into the market by buying up hundreds of millions of dollars of stock. In a sense, the old boys' network remains among these influential families, but they are a practical and internationally minded body, not local, and hardly smug.

There are perhaps eight or ten families whose names and businesses dominate corporate life in Hong Kong: Li Ka-shing (Cheung Kong Holdings), Raymond, Thomas and Walter Kwok

(Sun Hung Kai), Lee Shau Kee (Henderson Land Development Co.), Cheng Yu-tung (New World Development), Gordon Wu (Hopewell Holdings), Peter Woo and the Pao family (Wheelock), Michael Kadoorie (China Light & Power), the Chan family (Hang Lung Development). These families, and perhaps a dozen others, have more power to affect life in the colony, and the international community's perception of life in the colony, than any other individual or group. The Governor may grab the headlines, but the bottom line is theirs.

The financial power of this group is reflected in the share value of their listed interests and in their ability to influence all sectors of the economy; by any measure this is staggering wealth and phenomenal power.

With the exception of the Kadoories, they are all Chinese, some originally from Shanghai, some from southern provinces, and some native to Hong Kong. They all share a distaste for the spotlight, and more than one explained this aversion by quoting a Chinese colloquialism, 'The fattest pig is slaughtered first.'

We will be examining the origin and nature of these fortunes later. It is important at this point, however, to underline two distinct features of this group: the importance of *guanxi*, or connections, and the character of the group itself. If they have all this power, and they do, then why don't they exercise it more openly, obviously and aggressively? Why are there no Ross Perots? Of course it has to do with being Chinese, and not North American.

This club is both extremely practical – the fattest pig is slaughtered first – and highly intuitive – Cheng Yu-tung's lucky licence plate 8888. The combination shows in the way they handle the buying and selling of shares.

There are two ways to judge a company's stock. The more practical investors analyse fundamentals; they study charts, reports, facts and figures to determine a company's true value before deciding to buy or sell. The intuitive, however, believe that the stock market has a life of its own, that it has cycles and tides and a mysterious physics that can be felt but never understood. Neither position is ever one hundred per cent correct. What is certain is that change always comes quickly and from unexpected angles in Hong Kong. There's not enough time to study fundamentals. These families have made their fortunes by placing their bets intuitively and then managing them pragmatically. The fact that the Hang Seng Index rose 115 per cent during twelve turbulent months under Governor Patten suggests that they feel the future is ultimately bright. But they do so in spite of Patten's reforms, not because of them. Most of this group have between ten and twenty-five per cent of their assets now invested in mainland China.

Guanxi – pronounced 'gwan-shee' – is the Chinese word for connections, and connections are essential for success in Hong Kong and China. The members of the first circle are held together by a traditional respect for the integrity of the family unit. Ultimate authority rests with the father, and sons – especially the eldest – are expected to follow in the father's footsteps. This circle connects with other circles of the extended families of the father and mother. These central spheres are then connected to others of blood relation or relation through marriage. Trusted business partners and acquaintances whose loyalty and virtue have been tested are also included, along with their families and extended relations. A genealogical chart of the prominent families in Hong Kong would show a remarkable interpenetration of blood and money. In the crucial matter of business referrals, the closer to the core family the reference comes from, the more important and powerful the reference. What is striking about this system is how much trust is invested in these references. If Li Ka-shing provides an introduction, one can expect to be accorded almost as much respect – and extended almost as much trust – as would be shown to Li Ka-shing. It is a system whose main advantage seems to be a shortening of the period of time between introduction and the commencement of business.

27

Most of the interviews we did were arranged with the help of high-level introductions. These introductions are also necessary when interviewing individuals of similar stature in the West. But in the West, there is always a ten-minute test period at the beginning of the interview. The subject wants to be sure you are worthy of his or her time. In Hong Kong, the fact that you can get through the door is proof enough of your worth.

Guanxi is a speeded-up system for establishing trust, and generally works well in the high-pressure, high-speed, ever-changing atmosphere of the colony. But it has dangers. It is essentially arbitrary. It means that whom you know can often get you further than what you know. And nepotism decides the upper management of most of the large family businesses. There is nothing unfair about this, as the family usually holds most of the shares – unless the gene pool happens to deliver a dud. Some of these families understand the dangers of the system and claim to have introduced a more enlightened and practical solution to succession. Here's how Frank Chao, President of the giant shipping line, Wah Kwong & Co., Ltd, puts it:

> *I don't want to force my children to do anything. If they are interested, I'll welcome them to join the company. But I would like them to develop their own abilities . . . One very important point which I can mention here: the Chinese family business never lasts longer than three or four generations. The reason? The father gives to his son, son gives to grandson, all the way down the line. But inside the family tree, if there is one person who is not capable, the whole system will collapse. So it is much better to use the European system. The family can still be the shareholders and have the controlling share. The Chief Executive, or the Chief Administrator – well, you just buy the best one you can find – and let him protect the family's interests. You don't need to have family members running the company. In this way, the family business can go on for generations . . . The old Chinese system continues: father to son, son to son, but it may not be the best way to continue your empire.*

28

THE LAST GOVERNOR . . . OR THE FIRST POLITICIAN?

British paternalism and the plenipotentiary power of an appointed British Governor were seen as appropriate and necessary for Hong Kong's first 150 years. Why are democratic reforms so important today? And what innate quality makes the British more benevolent dictators than the Chinese? It seems patronizing and condescending to view the people of Hong Kong as helpless without British rule or a Western democratic system. But the last Governor of the last British-led administration is determined to bring greater democracy to the government of Hong Kong.

He apparently believes increased democracy will provide the people of Hong Kong with greater control over their destiny after 1997. But in Article 68 of The Basic Law, the Chinese have stated that, 'The ultimate aim is the election of all the members of the Legislative Council by universal suffrage.' The Chinese are as good as any nation at holding to agreements and treaties. Does Patten think they are lying? It is more likely that he is playing politics in an arena accustomed to the quiet shuffle of diplomacy.

The role and style of the Governor of Hong Kong has evolved more over the past few decades than any other aspect of the administration. This has as much to do with the evolution of Hong Kong into one of the world's great cities as it does with the politically complex and charged nature of its return to mainland China rule in 1997. Traditionally, the Governor was elevated from the upper ranks of the colonial service. But in 1971, he was chosen from the foreign services. Murray MacLehose had been Britain's Ambassador to Saigon and then to Copenhagen. He had some knowledge of Hong Kong as he had spent some time in the colony as a political advisor to the government. MacLehose began the change in demeanour of the Governor. He toured the colony and spoke with the ordinary citizens in the street. In 1982, MacLehose was succeeded by Sir Edward Youde, who was also from the Foreign Office and had been British Ambassador to Beijing. The selection of the Governor was clearly moving towards those who saw Hong Kong in an international context and whose experience qualified them for the coming negotiations for the return to mainland China rule. Youde could read Chinese and speak Mandarin. He had been party to delicate negotiations with the Chinese when he argued successfully for the release of the British frigate HMS *Amythst* in 1949. He was known as a passionate defender of Hong Kong's interests, but his term and impact were cut short when he died suddenly in his sleep while on a trip to Beijing in 1986.

David Wilson was also from the Foreign Office and had handled Hong Kong's interests while in Whitehall. Wilson brought a scholarly touch to the role, as he had left the Foreign Office for a number of years to complete a PhD and edit the scholarly journal, *The China Quarterly*. Wilson also read Chinese and spoke Mandarin. It seemed likely that Wilson would be the last Governor. He seemed a perfect choice: a scholar, a diplomat, a man fluent in the language of the mainland and highly educated in the history and culture of China. The specifics of Wilson's departure are unclear, but it is safe to assume that fallout from the massacre in Tiananmen Square in 1989, and a change in British domestic politics, combined to bring his term to an end in 1992.

In the wake of Tiananmen, the British government decided that construction of a new airport would help restore international confidence in Hong Kong's future after 1997. But such a massive project would have to involve the co-operation of mainland authorities. The airport would not be completed before 1997, so loan guarantees and contracts would have to have the approval of Beijing if creditors hoped to receive payments after that time. The years following Tiananmen saw most Western nations keeping a cool distance from the Beijing government. In this environment, Wilson's efforts to promote the airport could not help but be humiliating to Britain, which was signing a Memorandum of Understanding at a time when the rest of the world was still damning China over the 1989 massacre.

The opportunity to remove Wilson came with John Major's surprise election victory in the spring of 1992. Chris Patten, Chairman of the Conservative Party and mastermind of the election victory, failed to win re-election in his Bath constituency. It is certain that Major would have brought Patten into his Cabinet had Patten won his seat; it is also highly likely that Major offered Patten a number of powerful and prestigious appointed positions to choose from, in gratitude for his loyal support and the success of Patten's political strategy. He chose Hong Kong.

The gradual transformation of the role and person of the Governor since 1971 comes to an end with Chris Patten. What kind of man is he and what is his agenda as Hong Kong's last Governor? He is first and foremost a political being. Tactically, he seems to be most comfortable and capable in a state of crisis. The crisis he has created (democratic reform) has energized the position it opposes (mainland sovereignty), and the convergence of the two has created a third crisis (loss of business confidence and China's refusal of further negotiations). He is the kind of politician who is convinced that only he has the ability to reach into a storm of chaos and pull out the magic solution. If his remarkable success with John Major's campaign of 1992 is any indication, then he might just be the perfect man for such a charged and changing place. But he is gambling for high stakes. If he succeeds, he will win the respect and admiration of much of the world. If he fails, six million will pay for his errors. Either way, the England he returns to in 1997 will be grateful for what will be deemed heroic acts in the cause of Western democracy.

Chris Patten took office in July of 1992. On 7 October he delivered a speech to the Legislative Council outlining his agenda and proposed reforms. His predecessors had always argued for Hong Kong's interests in a manner that was designed not to offend or alienate China. This was not to be Patten's approach. It is possible that John Major felt that he had bowed to China's will in travelling to Beijing in July 1991 to sign the Memorandum of Understanding over the new

29

airport, and that this accommodation had brought him nothing but humiliation. What was left to be lost with a more confrontational position?

Accordingly, he set out aggressively to impose reforms on Hong Kong's three-tier system of government. The Governor is the head of the government and the representative of the Queen in Hong Kong. Supporting the Governor, and functioning as his Cabinet, is the Executive Council, comprising three ex-officio members (those who by their status alone warrant inclusion): the Chief Secretary (also deputy Governor), the Financial Secretary and the Attorney General. There are also ten additional members appointed by the Governor.

The first tier or the central body of the government is the Legislative Council of sixty members. Again, there are three ex-officio members: the Chief Secretary, the Financial Secretary and the Attorney General. Of the remaining fifty-seven members, eighteen are appointed by the Governor and thirty-nine are elected. Of the elected members, twenty-one are elected by what are called 'functional constituencies'. There are fifteen of these, made up of leading members of specific sectors of the community, including the medical profession, the legal profession and various economic and social sectors. Each functional constituency chooses the members it sends to the Legislative Council through direct, though strictly internal, elections. The final eighteen members are elected in an almost Western democratic style, through direct elections in specific geographical constituencies throughout the territory.

The second tier of the government is made up of the Urban and Regional Councils. The Urban Council is responsible for the provision of municipal services to the urban sectors, heavily populated areas such as Hong Kong and Kowloon (the total population of all urban areas is 3.2 million). The Regional Council is the municipal authority for the New Territories (population 2.6 million). Members of the Urban Council or the Regional Council represent specific geographic constituencies and are elected by registered voters of legal voting age.

The third tier of government is made up of the eighteen District Boards. The main purpose of the District Boards is to provide a forum for public consultation and participation. The District Boards in turn advise the government on the needs or concerns of the people living and working in the districts.

The basic purpose of Patten's reforms is to ensure that Hong Kong has a 'vigorous and effective', executive-led government accountable to the Legislature. This seems reasonable enough, but Patten's definition of 'vigorous and effective' includes a broadening of the participation of the whole community, or greater voter participation in the sitting members of the Legislative Council. This move towards greater democratization has caused the greatest controversy. He has also lowered the voting age from twenty-one to eighteen, making even greater numbers eligible to participate. And there are no more appointed members on the Municipal Councils or the District Boards, all are now selected through direct election. It is not as if the Chinese disagree with the concept of universal suffrage; the controversy stems from opposing interpretations of the Joint Declaration of 1984. The Chinese believe that Patten is violating the spirit of the accord; Patten argues that the changes he proposes do not encroach upon the specifics of that document. From a strictly legal point of view, Patten's position is untenable. If a contract is brought to court under dispute, it is the specific wording, and not the intent behind the writing of the contract, that is considered and judged. But international treaties, like the Joint Declaration, would be examined according to the original intent of the two parties, and not strictly by the wording of the final document signed by both parties. It also must have seemed to China that the movement of the return of Hong Kong to Chinese control in 1997 had changed to a restructuring of Hong Kong into an independent, sovereign state. The controversy and paranoia have increased in proportion to the growing lack of direct communication and consultation between China and Great Britain.

Patten is also making changes that ultimately enhance his own powers. Traditionally, new government policy would be put forward in a green paper, a document to be studied and debated in public. Following this consultative process, and accommodating public and official response, a white paper would be prepared outlining the government's final position on the matter. The white paper would then be brought before the Legislative Council for a vote. Patten has replaced this gradual, open process with a more presidential style, using his advisors and 'Cabinet', or Executive Council, to prepare the government's policy and announcing it publicly shortly before being brought before the Legislative Council for debate and vote.

Patten prohibited members of the Legislative Council from also sitting on the Executive Council. This eliminated the effect that interfering high-profile members of the Legislative Council might have had on the development of the Governor's policies. Further, he moved to appoint less well-known or well-connected citizens to the Legislative Council. Both of these changes reduce the influence of business-oriented members of the Legislative Council. This seems more democratic, but it also serves to distance the Governor from the direct pressure of the powerful businessmen whose influence is so very strong in Hong Kong society.

Finally, the Governor wished to broaden and expand the functional constituencies, so that they would be more representative of the whole working population, and not simply its most highly skilled members. These democratic reforms seem modest and hardly worthy of the controversy that surrounds them. After all, it is not as if Patten is suggesting that all sixty members of the Legislative Council be elected through a traditional Western-style general election. But the controversy doesn't stem from opposition to democracy, it stems from the way he has gone about it. A political animal, he still does not understand the politics of Hong Kong.

What will be the lasting effects of Patten's reforms? Will he really bring greater democracy to the colony as a kind of miraculous armour against the evils of Communist rule? Not likely. It won't take an innocent to discover that the emperor has no clothes. And the international headlines describing his confrontations with China will all soon fade from memory. One issue may be the precedent he has set for a future chief executive also to interpret freely the rules of the game to serve very different – and perhaps less morally compelling – goals.

ANSON CHAN
THE CHIEF SECRETARY

If it is easy to find fault with Patten's political agenda, it is nearly impossible to criticize his appointment of Anson Chan as Chief Secretary. Perhaps he chose *too* well, as newspaper polls almost always rank her popularity well above his.

In the past few years, no public figure has grown so much in stature, influence and regard as has Anson Chan. We first interviewed her while she was Secretary for Economic Services, spoke to her about her appointment as Secretary of the Civil Service, and were thrilled at the announcement of her appointment as Chief Secretary.

The first impression one has of Anson Chan is of formidable intellect, and powerful force of personality. This is not someone to treat lightly, or underestimate. But this armour soon gives way to a subtle femininity, and a deeply caring human being. She is shy, and highly intuitive. She uses her rigorous, almost aggressive intelligence, and what can become an icy demeanour, to protect or defend herself. Her eyes are quick and all-seeing. She uses language better than any of our subjects, but more importantly, she understands the subtleties and ambiguities of the language she hears; power comes from knowledge, and knowledge from listening well. She controls her smile, and releases it only reluctantly; it seems to want to show more than she will allow. The mouth expresses the only tension in the face, the only place where there is a struggle for greater expression of feeling. She can control the smile, but as Snowdon's portrait shows, the dimples give her away.

We have had closer contact with Anson Chan over the past few years than with anyone else in the colony. She has become a close friend and an enthusiastic supporter of this book. That is not to say that she agrees with the views we express – especially concerning the Governor, government policy, or the future of Hong Kong. She is loyal and discreet and has declined to read the manuscript until the book is available to the general public. She does not wish to influence our ideas. Chan is acutely aware of the responsibilities of her role, and of her position in Hong Kong society. She also understands how to allow

32

THE WORK ETHIC

We don't have the familiar provision of welfare that you have in the West. And so everybody in Hong Kong realizes that ultimately they have to rely on themselves. They can't rely on the state. That knowledge has been very conducive to cultivating a work ethic in Hong Kong.

Anson Chan

friendship and affection to grow amongst peoples – or nations – of differing opinions.

Anson Chan's father died when she was a child, and her mother left the children with relatives so that she could pursue her studies in Europe. Chan, being the eldest (by a few minutes over her twin sister Ninson), assumed the role of head of the family. It is a role she has never fully relinquished. And over the years, as brothers and sister have married or moved away, every opportunity is taken to bring the siblings together over meals or mahjong. When we were in Hong Kong we were often invited to join Anson Chan, her siblings and mother, for Sunday brunch or mid-week dinner. Tuesday nights are usually reserved for ballroom dancing. Her sister Ninson is proprietor of a ballroom dancing studio. This is one of her smaller interests; she is founder and CEO of the third largest travel agency in the colony. The family – the two sisters and whatever brothers are free – gather at a Shanghainese restaurant for dinner before going to the studio to dance. On some evenings Fang Zhaoling, the matriarch of the clan, is persuaded to join the family. Fang is a quiet, dignified woman. Her most striking features are her eyes – which miss nothing – and her hair, which she has allowed to grow grey. Most Hong Kong women, and almost all the men, begin colouring their hair at the first sign of grey. Her eyes are striking because they see everything, and comment on what they see. They take in information, and shine back a palpable emotional response.

Chan is solicitous, affectionate and respectful of her mother, now eighty-two. She takes charge over her mother's needs and addresses her as 'Mummy'. This does not sound at all infantile, or ingratiating, because it springs from a deep-felt respect for the primacy of the role of the mother, and is consistent with one who goes out of her way to draw the family together at every possible occasion. In Anson Chan's world, the family is the central core from which all else grows and to which all returns.

THE MARKET FORCE

This government has never attempted to set the pace, or tell industries in which areas they should invest, and in which areas they should do more research. We adopted the market force, by and large, simply because, long ago, we had decided that we don't have the ability to influence the world market. We have to depend on somebody in order to trade. We firmly believe that the marketplace is the best way to allocate resources. The resources of Hong Kong are limited anyway. If you look at the manufacturing industry, many of the manufacturing processes have already moved across the border. Why? Because land is scarce in Hong Kong. We are not going to compete with China, with its vast reservoir of cheap land and the abundance of labour. That process of relocation from Hong Kong to China has already been ordained by the market force. If the private entrepreneurs decided to do it, they would do it. The government has nothing to do with it. That is the gist of our policy.

Anson Chan

At the end of the meal it is Fang Zhaoling who rises first from the table. She bids us goodnight and is escorted home by one of her sons. The rest of us take a lift up to the dance studio, a few floors above the restaurant.

Archie Chan, Anson Chan's husband of thirty-three years, has declined to join us this evening. Archie Chan is a top executive with Caltex Oil, and Commandant of the colony's 5,000-strong auxiliary police force. The Chans have a daughter and a son and two grandchildren. Anson Chan explains that her husband loves to dance and has a natural musicality and grace, but abhors the constriction of tutored steps.

Tuesday nights are open practice night at the academy. Many of Hong Kong's most distinguished citizens are assembled to fine tune their footwork, including Baroness Dunn and tycoon Peter Woo. But attention this night is focused on three anonymous couples. They dance

LESSONS OF HISTORY

**When foreign powers invaded China, the Chinese were forced into
concluding the unequal treaties with Britain, ceding Hong Kong to the
invaders. This has not been forgotten. Above all, China's leaders have a
great fear that if political reform were introduced into China prematurely,
it would lead to chaos. If you look around at what happened in Eastern
Europe, in Russia, Yugoslavia, you can't blame them. What has so-called
democracy brought to these countries except misery, high inflation,
factional war, and all the atrocities?**

Anson Chan

beautifully and confidently, and so well that we wonder why they might need a practice night.
Chan explains that they are from the mainland, probably Shanghai, and adds that ballroom
dancing has always been popular among Beijing's ruling class . . .

The Chief Secretary is the second most powerful position in the government, and in the
event of the Governor's absence or incapacitation, she is deputized with all the powers of the
Governor's office. She, the Financial Secretary and the Attorney General are the principal
advisors to the Governor. It is the duty of the Chief Secretary to formulate government policies,
and ensure their effective implementation. She is CEO of a civil service of 190,000, and head of
the Government Secretariat, a governing body made up of the secretaries of each branch of
government and their immediate staffs. She is also the Senior Official Member of the Executive
Council and the Legislative Council.

Her power works two ways. One is the direct, bureaucratic decision-making path, where
permits are issued, or refused, licences granted, or not, control over the thousands of details
that bear on a business-driven economy. The other lies in her connections, both in Hong Kong
and in China. Both will be affected by
what happens after the mainland
takes control. China may dismiss
many top officials appointed by Britain
and replace them with mainland
Chinese, or Hong Kong citizens who
have demonstrated sympathy for the
mainland cause. Mrs Chan has
expressed a desire to remain at her
post until the expiration of her term in
1999. Will China keep her? Our guess
is yes. But there are lingering
questions. All Chief Secretaries have
been knighted within a year or so of
assuming office. How might this dusty
stamp of the British Establishment
affect her chances? If the British don't
offer her the title, they will seem

36

racist, sexist, or both. If she refuses it, she will appear to be currying favour with her future masters. Probably she will accept the title with the grace that is her trademark, but decline to use it publicly. It will not appear on her letterhead or on public documents, and she will discourage people from addressing her as Dame Anson Chan.

But how might China view one of their own who has worked so hard to rise to the top of the British-trained civil service? In all likelihood, China will see Chan as Chinese first, and loyal employee second. In public and private, she is unwavering in her support for the Governor. If she shows such loyalty to this master, then she is just as likely to show equal loyalty to the next. She has many enduring and significant ties to the mainland. Her grandfather, an influential industrialist, was assassinated in 1925, and her mother, Fang Zhaoling, is considered one of the masters of contemporary Chinese painting. (Sotheby's recently auctioned one of her paintings for HK $750,000, approximately US $100,000). Victoria House, the Chief Secretary's official residence at 15 Barker Road, is filled with her dark atmospheric work.

But the most compelling question about Anson Chan is not whether or not she will remain on the 'through train', but if she will be chosen by Beijing as Hong Kong's first Chief Executive. We had witnessed an example of how she is regarded outside this community in 1994, when she made her first official visit to Canada. We offered to drive her to St Catharines, Ontario to visit an uncle. Before returning to Toronto, we made a brief detour to Niagara Falls. And a number of times as we strolled among the Thanksgiving crowds, a Chinese family – whether visitors or new Canadians was never clear – would stop and stare. Each time the same respectful ritual was observed. They would send the eldest male forward, he would bow slightly and offer the family's respects. She is accustomed to such attention at home, but to see it shown half a world away speaks of how highly she is regarded by all Chinese.

There is no guarantee that the mainland authorities want or appreciate a civil servant who is instantly recognized and treated with such deference abroad. However, the admiration shown to her by London, Washington and the world community, assure that her voice will be listened to carefully in the months leading up to 1 July 1997. The Governor will leave, Anson Chan will stay. But in what capacity, and under what terms?

The confidence of connections makes it possible for Anson Chan to meet regularly and privately with men as powerful as Li Ka-shing. Eyebrows are not raised as they might be in the West, where behind-closed-doors meetings between business tycoons and top bureaucrats ring alarm bells, and provoke concerns that secret deals are being struck. Here, the assumption is that connections do not exist without honour; to lose honour or face is to lose everything of lasting value, and therefore, when Anson Chan dines privately with Li Ka-shing, nothing dishonourable will be done. Moreover, in this city-village, it is virtually impossible to keep the circling powers from encountering each other.

CHINA AND DEMOCRACY

In its entire civilization, China has never had democracy as we know it. So, in many ways, democracy is a strange word. I think you have to ask yourself what is meant by it. Does it mean one-man-one-vote, or does it mean enjoying the basic freedom that you take advantage of in the Western world? In China, they have not even tasted basic freedom, let alone one-man-one-vote. In China, or in Hong Kong, come to that, if you ask people about what matters to them most, it is the ability to have equality of opportunity and employment, furthering their education, the ability to enjoy the quality of life, basic freedom, the freedom of speech, or worship, the freedom to travel. These are the things that matter. Now suppose you ask them at the same time, 'Would you like more representative government, would you like to have one-man-one-vote?' Yes, the answer must be yes. But if you go on to say, 'You have to pay a price for that,' the answer will be different, depending on what price you are going to extract out of them.

Anson Chan

LI KA-SHING

He agreed to the interview reluctantly, and because Baroness Dunn had introduced us. We were told he would give us precisely one hour, and that the interview had to be conducted in Cantonese. He showed the same standoffishness he would later employ with Lord Snowdon.

We arrive at the China Building, 29 Queen's Road Central, well in advance of the appointed time, 3.30pm. We take the lift to the floor we have been given. When the lift doors open, we find ourselves facing a serious-looking, blue-blazered security guard. He uses a mobile phone to call and confirm our appointment and then leans into the lift and punches a button to a higher floor. Again, we rise. When the doors open we are greeted by two more guards, equally serious. We do not feel encouraged to step out of the lift until a very petite, young woman appears between them and addresses us personally. The guards seem to melt away and we find ourselves facing a reception desk with a semi-circular staircase climbing up behind it. We are led up these stairs by Amy Au, the young woman who has saved us from the security guards, and who is Li Ka-shing's current Executive Assistant. Li later explains to us that he has had only five such assistants in his long career and that all are still with his organization. The eldest of these assistants, and the first, is now in his eighties and sits on the board of the flagship company, Cheung Kong Holdings. One would think that Au would have to have passed rigorous examinations, or be extremely well connected, or had graduated with honours from Princeton, Harvard and Oxford in order to be trusted with such an important position. But the truth is that she simply responded to a newspaper advertisement for a position at Cheung Kong and worked for a time with a pool of secretaries until this position became available and she was interviewed by Li for the job.

After a few minutes of trying to settle our nerves and get our bearings, Au leads us down a narrow corridor to Li's office. The tone of the office is set by dark, stained panelling. Li's desk faces the door of the office at an angle; his chair places him in the protective shelter of a corner of the building. We are invited to sit on one of two black leather sofas arranged around a modern glass table. To the left of the door, around a corner, are a table and chairs that look as if they serve as both

WALKING FAST

In the late 1950s, when I made my first trip to New York City, I was struck by how quickly people walked in the streets. In Hong Kong in those days, people walked very very slowly. At least compared to New York. But today, today in Hong Kong they walk faster than anywhere else in the world.

Li Ka-shing

a dining table and an intimate meeting space. There are no papers or files or books or pens on his desk. There are no traces of business having been transacted, or negotiations in progress. And, during our time with him, he will receive only one phone call, which concerns questions about a lease on an office building and lasts no more than thirty seconds. The most striking feature in the office is a bank of four televisions arranged against the wall facing his desk. Three of these show views of the approach to his office: the lift, the waiting room and the hall. A popular Chinese soap opera is playing on the fourth.

Unless he is on the golf course, Li Ka-shing is almost always seen in a dark blue suit, white shirt and conservative tie. He has a white handkerchief in the breast pocket of his jacket. He takes great pride in telling us that the suit he is wearing is at least ten years old and that the quartz watch he has worn for years cost only $50. But this is perhaps a kind of reverse snobbism. The man who can afford anything going out of his way to show the common touch. It is also a kind of uniform. It hides personality behind the look of the common man. But it has the opposite effect of what he intends. It makes us wonder what he really cares about, what his tastes are and what he feels compelled to hide.

His handshake is firm and forthright, his glance direct, he is cool, even severe. He motions for us to sit. The obligatory tea is sent for. The door is closed. Amy Au sits opposite with a note pad and tape recorder. Li wants to know what we want. It is not a friendly or inviting question. He begins speaking in Cantonese. But after a few questions he starts to relax, and after five minutes he switchs back to English. He says it isn't fair to speak in Cantonese since one of us (Lawrence Jeffery) cannot understand. His only condition is that we ensure that his language is reproduced as grammatically correct. This is a man obsessed with detail and appearances. Simon Murray, the former head of Hutchison Whampoa, the old British trading house or hong that Li took over in 1979, told us that the man's genius is in his ability to absorb, retain and fully understand the finest points of the most complicated contracts. Nothing is left to chance. At least nothing within his direct control or influence.

This extraordinary precision of observation and analysis gives the impression of a thoroughly rational and Western man. He understands the language of Western business. He knows the customs, costume and code of behaviour better than anyone we met. He confounds

expectations by acting more British than the British, but he is Chinese. He changed the time of his mother's funeral because a *feng shui* expert said it was a more propitious time. He has a Confucian awe for scholarship and the artist. He gives millions of dollars to universities and to build schools in China. And he tells us several times that one of his hobbies is to read books. Many books, all kinds of books; we are not to view him as a businessman only concerned with the bottom line, a soulless greed machine.

He knows he is being watched, and he cares about what we see. But the armour isn't there to hide or protect something, it's not a disguise or diversion: the surface is the substance. Li Ka-shing was born in 1928 in Chiu Chow (Swatow), a city not far up the mainland coast from Hong Kong. It was the death of his father, and responsibility for providing for his family, that ignited his remarkable drive:

> *The most difficult time in my life was when my father passed away. I was only fourteen years old. My father had a good education, and he was very intelligent, but he had nothing to leave his three children, no money at all. He thought the only thing he could leave me was knowledge, so he asked if there was anything I wanted to ask him . . . I told him not to worry. I said, 'Soon you will be better, and one day our family will be outstanding.' I knew he was going to die. The doctor had told me he only had a week to live. He had TB. At that time many died from it, especially if you were poor and could only go to the government hospital. But at that time I already had the confidence that one day I would succeed. I had come to Hong Kong with my family when I was twelve years old, in 1940. I was already quite mature. Neither my father nor my mother needed to discipline me, I knew what I had to do . . .*

He began his business career as a teenager:

> *When I was seventeen years old I was a wholesaler, a salesman. The company had seven salesmen, and then the boss decided to change the policy for the annual bonus. Before, everybody got more or less the same and the bonus was tied to overall sales. Now he said we would get a bonus according to how much each salesman sold. It was a mistake. My sales were the highest and seven times more than the second best. You know how I did it? I was in the office and on the phone selling before anyone. I never stopped. And at night, when the others went to dinner, to movies, or to play mahjong, I was still there, working. The factory was in production around the clock. I was always there making sure my orders were processed correctly, that the merchandise was right and that my customers were always happy.*
>
> *After a while, people only wanted to deal with me, because I gave them the best service. They didn't want to buy from anybody else . . . So when the boss said the bonus would be based on sales, I knew there would be trouble. If they paid me according to sales, my income would have been higher than the general manager's. So I told the boss to pay me*

HONG KONG'S FORMULA

I think the reason we are so successful in Hong Kong is because we have no choice. You must work hard. As you know, we have no natural resources. We are six million people in a very small area. Our only resource, and our strength, is our ability to work hard. We also believe that tomorrow will be better. We work towards a better tomorrow.

A BILLIONAIRE'S SIMPLE LIFE

I like a simple life. I like simple food. I enjoy vegetables. I don't enjoy fancy dinner parties; ninety per cent of the time, I turn down invitations, unless it's something very meaningful. If I'm needed, if they want me there, then of course I'll go . . . But usually everyone talks nonsense and after the party I feel very lonely. I spend my time working, non-stop, in Hong Kong and in China, too. Of course, I can't keep working for ever. Sooner or later, I'll have to retire. Except for philanthropy, education and medical health – I can do that kind of work for ever.

Li Ka-shing

REPUTATION

You have to develop a name, a good, solid name, and if you do, the fortune will follow. It's difficult if all you want to do is make lots of money, if all you're doing is chasing after money. But money comes to you if you have a good name, in part because people like to associate with you, and do business with you . . . If you concentrate on your name, your reputation, the rest will follow.

Li Ka-shing

what the next highest salesman was getting. I was seventeen. I had nice clothes, cufflinks, a watch, everything I needed. I didn't need more . . . And you mustn't be greedy. And when I was eighteen another company offered me a lot of money to go with them. They knew how good I was. But I turned them down. I knew what I wanted. I'd made up my mind. When the time was right I was going to start my own business . . .

Li founded Cheung Kong Holdings in 1950, with personal savings of HK $50,000. He was twenty-two. The name of the company is inspired by the Yangtze, a great river made from the contributions of many smaller sources. He says that he never took a day off, or a holiday, for the first ten years. His first great success came with the manufacture of plastic flowers, a great novelty at the time; and he was so successful that he was chartering cargo jets to fly the product out of Hong Kong.

He had made his first million by the late 1950s. He then began his move into property development. It was the only resource in Hong Kong that was limited and that was sure to become even more valuable. The population of Hong Kong had not stopped growing since the Communists closed the border in 1949. It was his astonishing ability to look at a piece of property, or an existing building, and see not only its true current value, but also its value after development that made him such a success. His near photographic memory of the smallest details and the implications of codes and contracts made it possible for him to make instant decisions. From the outside, his moves appeared inspired by instinct, but they were almost always the result of homework, hours of study and analysis, and a quicksilver mind. By the late 1970s, he was becoming famous for his business success and wealth and began to take centre stage with the other tycoons of his generation.

In 1979, Li bought what was in effect a controlling stake in Hutchison Whampoa. Hutchison was one of the few remaining British hongs founded in the nineteenth century. Swires and Jardines boast a similar history, but remain in British control. This was a psychological as well as a financial coup, as Li was the first Chinese to take control of such an Establishment firm.

The acquisition of Hutchison Whampoa signalled the beginning of a diversification of Li's interests. Hutchison had some property holdings but was also involved in trading, warehousing, quarrying, cargo and container handling, engineering and retailing. Their retailing interests included the Park 'n' Shop chain of supermarkets and Watson's drugstore chain.

The early eighties were a quiet time for Li as property prices fell and business consolidated. In 1985, he continued his diversification with the purchase of 33.8 per cent of the Hongkong Electric Company. He also announced the investment of HK $4 billion in the Whampoa Garden residential complex. This huge development on the Kowloon side of the harbour suggested Li's confidence in Hong Kong's future and signalled another property boom.

In 1986, Li moved abroad in a big way when he bought a controlling stake in Husky Oil, Canada's largest oil and gas company. This move led to a certain amount of speculation that he was lining up overseas investments in democratic countries as a hedge against 1997. Others were concerned that he was now moving into areas where he had little expertise or experience.

In 1987, Li restructured part of his business empire. Cavendish International was set up to hold all the non-electricity-related interests of Hongkong Electric. Li wanted to assure consumers and shareholders that the electric company's profits came from its function as a utility, and that no funds were being diverted to or from other interests. The electric company was also open to public scrutiny and political pressure; separating the interests allowed more liberty in the management and financing of the other holdings.

In late 1987, Li joined with a group of investors to win the rights to develop the Vancouver Expo site on Canada's west coast. This comprised 203 acres in the centre of British Columbia's largest city. There was considerable local controversy as the total price was only C $320 million and the value upon completion is expected to be C $2 billion. Li also increased his personal holdings in the Canadian Imperial Bank of Commerce, Canada's largest bank in terms of assets, to almost ten per cent, just under the limit allowed by the Canadian Bank Act. He told us that he would buy more if only they would let him. In 1994, the CIBC's richest year in history, it showed a profit of $1.4 billion.

By 1995, Li was firmly established as one of the outstanding businessmen of the world. Now, his attention turns to 1997.

He is confident that Hong Kong's return to China will bring only greater prosperity. He was a member of the Basic Law Drafting Committee which drew up the constitution under which Hong Kong will be governed. He is also a member of the Preliminary Working Committee, a group of influential Hong Kong citizens selected by Beijing to help advise on transitional matters. He says:

> *China has great potential, it will go far. And I am truly committed to its success. When I commit to something, I always keep my word. I always honour the promises I make . . . My present commitment to China represents twenty per cent of the total assets of my company. And that will grow . . . Today, we are partners with the Shanghai government for the whole container terminal. This is a completely new idea, a new concept. A complete container terminal. We're also in the property business in China, many different kinds of projects. And it's possible we will also become involved in the energy business. I mean the construction of a power station. This would mean a huge investment, of course. We're also involved in joint ventures with manufacturers. And eventually we hope to become partners in other key industries inside China . . .*

43

As crucial as what will happen in the immediate years after 1997 is what will happen to Li's vast and expanding empire once he leaves the helm. He is a widower, whose wife died suddenly and tragically in 1990. His two sons, Victor and Richard, began attending company directors' meetings when they were ten and eight, respectively. Now thirty and twenty-eight, they are assuming more and more control over ever-larger chunks of the conglomerate, but it is far from certain that they will inherit. They are still young; they have still to prove themselves; they will follow their father's wishes, whatever that implies.

Li said he would give us precisely one hour, but the interview has lasted more than two hours. As we get up to leave, he points to a large soapstone Inuit carving and reminds us that it, too, came from Canada. It is the only piece of art in the office, and clearly something he likes. He sends Amy on an errand, and walks us down the corridor to the waiting room. Amy returns carrying two large books which his companies have played a part in sponsoring, photographic essays on China, and he offers them as parting gifts.

CONFIDENCE

You must have a strong base to work from. You must be confident, but not too confident. You must have confidence in order for others to have confidence in you. For this, you must know yourself. Now, this is a very difficult thing. To know somebody is difficult, but to know yourself is even more difficult.

Li Ka-shing

BARONESS DUNN

In May 1995 it was revealed that Li Ka-shing had set up three linked trusts in George Town, Grand Cayman, to hold his personal shares in Cheung Kong Holdings. When questioned, he explained that he had set up the trusts to avoid punishing inheritance taxes, and not because of any loss of confidence in Hong Kong's future. And in June 1995, Baroness Dunn announced that she would be leaving Hong Kong at the end of the year to become an executive director of the Swire Group in London. Both announcements shook public confidence in Hong Kong's future. And then in early July, just before the book was to go to press, it was announced that Anson Chan had made a secret three-day trip to Beijing. The Hong Kong stock market shot up 400 points. This is Hong Kong – an ever-changing landscape – volatile, unpredictable and yet, after every apparent setback, bouncing back higher still.

Lydia Dunn's power grew from the remarkable success of her business career with Swire's, one of the oldest British trading houses in the colony. She was, until Anson Chan became Chief Secretary, the most powerful woman in the colony, and the first woman, and the first Chinese, elevated to the British House of Lords (in 1990). (Lord Kadoorie, 1899–1993, of China Light & Power and the Peninsula Hotel, was the first Hong Kong-born citizen elevated to the House of Lords in 1981.)

We conducted the interview in her office at Swire House. When we arrived, her white Cadillac with white leather interior was idling at the side door of the building. It is oddly ostentatious – not a particularly expensive car, and the type of car one sees on the road in North America all the time, but it is probably the only white Cadillac on Hong Kong Island.

Baroness Dunn (Dunn is a Westernized spelling of her Chinese maiden name, Deng) is one of Hong Kong's most glamorous, elegant and beautiful women. She is also one of its most accomplished citizens.

AN ORIENTAL NEW YORK

Hong Kong could be said to be in the middle of being transformed from an Oriental London into an Oriental New York. Until recently, its role as a business centre has, like London's, been disproportionate to the size of the domestic economy, and heavily international and trade oriented. But Hong Kong is in the process of becoming the business centre to a massive and dynamic continental economy on whose coast it sits – the role New York has played in the development of the United States.

Baroness Dunn

She is a Director of John Swire & Sons (Hong Kong) Limited, Deputy Chairman of the Hongkong and Shanghai Banking Corporation, a Director of Cathay Pacific Airways and a member of the AB Volvo International Advisory Board. Politically, she is the Senior Member of the Executive Council. In this capacity, she plays a significant role in the administration of Hong Kong, the formulation of government policies and the enactment of legislation.

She was born in Hong Kong on 29 February 1940 into an upper-class business family. She was a boarder at St Paul's convent school in Hong Kong, where she met and became friends with Anson Chan, born one day earlier. There were only about fifty boarders, and few Chinese. She led a very sheltered life until she left Hong Kong to go to university in California. She says the cultural shock occurred when she returned to Hong Kong after four years of study in the United States, and she declined to join the family firm.

My father was a banker and trader in Shanghai. He continued trading and started a printing company when we moved to Hong Kong. My mother's family had been one of the biggest tea merchants in China. I wanted to work and they encouraged me to work, and they fully understood that I didn't want to join the family business. I just didn't feel I would get the proper training. I wanted to go to a major company, non-Chinese, which had a more structured corporate culture.

She joined Swire's, a trading house founded in the nineteenth century, and one of the few still in British hands.

I was very lucky – timing helps! I started at a time when the Hong Kong economy was taking off. Firms were looking for properly trained professionals, so I joined at the right time, and as a result I moved up very quickly.

46

She dismisses the problems of chauvinism or sexism, saying,

I don't think many women in Hong Kong face that many problems working with men, because people are just too busy making money to worry about it. Do they want a woman to

STREET SCENE

One evening in London, I had arranged to meet up with Sir S. Y. Chung and other members of Hong Kong's Executive Council for a Chinese meal in Soho, after a visit to No 10 Downing Street. I dressed smartly for the evening, took a taxi to Gerrard Street and found that I was the first to arrive. It was a warm evening. I waited on a street corner under a lamp-post, swinging my handbag, in my very high-heeled shoes. After being circled once or twice by some very good-looking men, a Middle Eastern gentleman came up to me and began to talk, just when Sir S. Y. got out of his taxi half a block away. Seeing what was happening, he broke into a run, waving the £5 note that he was about to pay the taxi driver and shouting all the way, 'She's mine, she's mine . . .'

Baroness Dunn

be manager of this big department? They look at your file, if it looks right, let's give her a try.
We need good people and that's been the mentality, and another reason why we're so
successful.

We were told that one of the first real signs that Lydia Dunn was going to have a brilliant
career came when she hired a man as her executive assistant. It showed audacity, if nothing
else.

She worked hard, and rocketed up through the ranks. She was the first Chinese to become a
managing director, and the first Chinese to sit on the main board of Swire's. Her career took
centre stage in her life until 1988, when she married a British lawyer, Michael Thomas, the
former Attorney General of Hong Kong.

She began her political career in the 1970s. She was first invited to participate on several
advisory boards and was then appointed to the Legislative Council in 1976. When we asked her
about the important moments in her political career she mentioned her efforts in 1989 to obtain
the right to settle in Britain for some of Hong Kong's citizens, those who may find life under the
Chinese insupportable.

I went to the foreign affairs committee and I just broke down and cried when we were arguing for British passports for Hong Kong citizens. This was after Tiananmen Square. The British Parliamentary foreign affairs committee had sent six people here to take evidence. I was one of those called. I know why I cried. I just felt a deep sense of humiliation for Hong Kong. Here is this vibrant place and these dynamic people. We made Hong Kong what it is today. I was sitting in front of six people who had control over our destiny. They gave me fifteen minutes. I was describing the plight of Hong Kong people running around the world trying to get a second passport. It's not because they want to leave, it's because they want to stay, they want that insurance policy. The poignancy of our situation was so stark that day, sitting there, you know sitting there facing these six people, I just, I think that was why I just wept . . .

She had to leave. Her car was waiting. But she asked us to join her later for a drink at her home.

It is rare in Hong Kong to be invited to someone's residence. There are approximately two hundred private, free-standing homes on Hong Kong Island, but most people live in flats

considered very small by Western standards. Socializing – even simply family gatherings – is usually done over meals in restaurants. So it is a rare privilege to be able to see how one of Hong Kong's most distinguished citizens lives.

The view of Hong Kong is breathtaking. The ceilings are twenty feet high and supported by walls of glass. All of Hong Kong lies at your feet. To the north, almost directly below, is the roof of the residence of the Governor; higher up, across the strait, glimmers Kowloon, and far in the distance the lights of the New Territories and the border of China.

And it is difficult to imagine a more beautiful home than the fabulous

> ## OUR FUTURE LIES WITH CHINA
> We in Hong Kong have seized the opportunities presented to us by the opening up of China's economy. We have been the driving force behind the spectacular growth in southern China over the past ten years. We shall continue to play a key role in the greater China economy in the years to come. We all know that our future lies with China.
> *Baroness Dunn*

penthouse she and her British husband have so carefully designed and decorated on the top floor of one of Hong Kong's most exclusive addresses. It is a home of exquisite surfaces and textures and deep rich colour. Exquisite surfaces do not imply superficiality. In Chinese art, the nature of the material is not disguised or hidden, it is seen as important to the overall appreciation of the work of art as the elegance of the craftsman's line, the richness of the ceramicist's palette, or the complexity and virtuosity of the sculptor's craft.

Baroness Dunn is quick to point out that an internationally respected decorator assisted her with her home. His greatest task must have been to co-ordinate her remarkable collection of Chinese art. It is difficult to rest one's eyes on anything without suddenly realizing that what one is looking at is something quite remarkable. But there is nothing casual or haphazard about the arrangement of these objects. Though each room is different in tone and colour from the next, all are flavoured by a selection of Baroness Dunn's collection of Chinese tomb figurines. When a person of substance died, it was traditional to place in the tomb ceramic miniatures of all those things that represented position in society, or that were important in life.

It is striking to see a priceless figurine, placed on a low table by a passageway, where a full skirt or long evening gown could easily catch and pull it to the floor. The Baroness would have it no other way. She wants to live with the objects and not simply appreciate them behind glass. But this seems to strike a deeper significance and reflect the Chinese character at the heart of one of Hong Kong's most Westernized citizens.

In the West, treasures are displayed in protective custody. By scattering hers in a seemingly casual manner about her home, Baroness Dunn is disguising their true aesthetic value. The eyes of the connoisseur will find them, the amateur might experience the pleasure of discovery, and the insensitive will remain blind.

This is a home designed for entertaining. What we see is meant to be seen. On her writing desk is a display of photographs of Lady Dunn with almost every member of Britain's Royal Family. It is difficult in this home to identify or find the private spaces and intimate corners where she and her husband are most comfortable. Around the corner from her desk is her husband's small study. The pictures he has chosen to display are only of her, or the two of them together. As we were to ask ourselves many times, what is the message, and who the audience?

49

MARTIN LEE
A MARTYR-TO-BE?

Martin Lee is the most high profile of all of Hong Kong's political figures. He is the sixth of seven children. His mother was visiting Hong Kong when he was born on 8 June 1938. Lee's father was a general in the Nationalist army and fought against the Communist forces until settling in Hong Kong in 1949, when mainland China had become unsafe for men like him.

Lee studied English Literature and Philosophy at the University of Hong Kong, before going on to London to read Law. He began practising law in Hong Kong in 1956, and was made a Queen's Counsel in 1979. He is a very successful barrister, who spent three years as Chairman of the Hong Kong Bar Association (1980–3). He admits to having enough assets outside of Hong Kong to provide for his wife and son should they be forced to leave. He lives well in a comfortable apartment on a fashionable street bearing the war-like name of Magazine Gap Road. A Jaguar and a BMW are parked in the garage. These are expensive cars anywhere in the world, but they bear an additional one hundred per cent import tax in the colony.

We are greeted at his office by a young American woman called Minky, who had been an assistant and speech writer for US Attorney General Richard Thornburg, a highly respected member of Ronald Reagan's government. When her time with Thornburg came to an end, she found her interest drawn to Martin Lee, of whom she had read in the US press. He was the only voice for democratic reform in Hong Kong that seemed able to attract the attention of international media, and she went to work for him.

He is a romantic figure. We can see Patten's stance as cynical and self-serving because he has every intention of leaving. Martin Lee states very clearly, and often, that he plans to stay. He has said that his martyrdom would serve his cause and his party, the United Democrats, well, give it focus and renewed energy. And focus and energy are perhaps what the party needs most these days. In 1991, Lee made international headlines when his party came out the clear winner in the first direct elections for seats in the Legislative Council. Of the eighteen seats (of sixty) to be filled by direct election, the United

50

Democrats won twelve. However, the novelty has worn off; membership in the party grew from only 627 in 1992 to 655 in 1993.

THE BEAR'S PALM AND THE FISH

I went to Beijing in 1982, as the leader of a group of lawyers and other people, and a delegation from the Hong Kong Macau Affairs Office came to see us, headed by Li Hou and Lu Ping. They said, 'Look, the leaders of China have considered it appropriate to take Hong Kong, Kowloon and the New Territories back in 1997, because that's what one of the three unequal treaties said. And it is unrealistic for Hong Kong to remain under British rule without the New Territories. We believe it's good for China, good for Hong Kong. What do you think?'

Of course, our faces dropped, and then Li Hou said, 'Don't be afraid! What we want to do is to change two things only, change the Governor, change the flag, that's all. Everything else will remain the same.'

I said, 'If you wish to take back Hong Kong's sovereignty, and at the same time you wish Hong Kong to remain prosperous, it's impossible. It's like the Chinese classical saying, "There are two delicacies, the bear's palm and the fish; both are delicacies and you can have one, but not both."'

Martin Lee

Minky is apologetic for the delay. Lee is either fighting the Legislative Council, or traffic in Central. But he will be here.

His office is a stage for the man. Offices are either decorated with the accumulated bits and pieces of a lifetime, the important things that stick; or they're instant offices – looking as if everything was bought at the same place on the same day, and if you look close enough you might find a sales sticker or a price tag. Martin Lee's office, however, with its dark floor-to-ceiling shelves laden with legal books, its heavy Victorian desk, its meeting table with the current day's newspaper clippings, is a scene set for a stern schoolmaster's lecture. It is not surprising to hear that he also holds press conferences here, and that he sits behind his desk or in front of a bank of legal books. He knows the effect and importance of gesture. He understands the sound bite and the visual bite that are the diet of international media.

When he enters, we stand. But we stand as if caught at something naughty, not just out of courtesy. He examines our faces and looks deeply into our eyes. We expect him to say, 'Well, what have you to say for yourselves this time?'

He is tall and thin, his face is angular and when he looks at you he peers through his glasses as if they were microscopes focusing an already intense and serious gaze to a penetrating force. He chooses his words carefully, and rarely needs more than a few words to hint at the direction you want him to take before he's off and after it. When he comes to the choice of a word that might summarize or climax a thought, he seems to taste it, rolling it over his tongue before delivering it across thin, drawn lips. He is precise, easy to listen to. He never uses the Western politician's clichés and tends to illustrate all his points with anecdotes from his life or from Chinese classical sayings.

Lee is not the only leader of a political party in Hong Kong; there are others, there are also independents, but Lee is the most visible, the most articulate, the most attractive to Western media and clearly the most determined politician around.

Lee was first elected to the Legislative Council by the legal functional constituency in 1985, after Beijing had appointed him as a member of the Basic Law Drafting Committee the year before. Lee's father warned him about the Communists, the Chinese Communists, saying that they like to make use of people:

He said it to my wife, and asked my wife to speak to me. Once they finish using you, they dump you. So my wife repeated it to me, we pillow talked. And she did it quite often, because my father did it again and again. So I sat down with the old man, and I said, look, this is what I feel. Of course they are making use of me, that's why they've appointed me to this Basic Law Drafting Committee. But that gives me an opportunity to really do something for Hong Kong, and I said I know of my own limitations, I know that the chances of implementing this policy – one country, two systems, and Hong Kong people ruling Hong Kong are not great . . . But then I know that if I don't even try, the chances are zero. So the old man was happy. As long as you know that the odds are great against you, and you are still willing to go for it, fine.

When Lee went to Beijing in 1987, as part of the Hong Kong delegation of the Basic Law Drafting Committee, they were greeted by Deng Xiaoping in the Great Hall of the People. Deng declared to the gathering that great prosperity lay ahead for all, and that the concept of one country, two systems, could be extended from fifty years to one hundred years. But when Deng went on to say that China will not allow Hong Kong to be turned into a breeding ground for dissent against China, and that Western-style democracy is inappropriate for Hong Kong, Martin Lee was enraged. Enraged and energized. He was scheduled to deliver a speech on legal principles the next day. He re-wrote his speech to reflect his state of mind and his continuing concerns for the people of Hong Kong:

> *What do you mean by people who love China or love Hong Kong? Do you mean people who would say things the leaders of China would like to hear? Or do you mean these are people who genuinely love Hong Kong and would say honest things about Hong Kong – although critical of the Chinese government?*

Martin Lee has not visited China since delivering that speech. He was considered a dangerous subversive from that day forward, although he did not form his own party at once. Lee argued to have one-quarter of the seats in the Legislative Council directly elected in the 1988 elections. But the colony's first direct elections did not come until 1991. In the spring of 1990, ten months after Tiananmen Square, Lee founded the United Democrats. Asked about two competitive political parties, he says, 'You've got one liberal party which is anything but liberal and one pro-Communist party, the Democratic Alliance for the Betterment of Hong Kong, which is anything but democratic.'

Lee was initially enthusiastic when Patten arrived on the scene. He was encouraged by the new Governor's efforts to expand democratic reforms in anticipation of the final elections under British rule to be held in 1995. But democratic reforms face more than China's disapproval. Many business leaders in the colony believe reforms will compromise Hong Kong's economic success. Vincent Lo, a young billionaire who recently left the political scene to return to his business interests, complained to us that democracy was a messy, uneven proposition: 'It's not business, there is no bottom line.'

When, near the end of the interview, we asked Martin Lee if he was worried about his safety when China does finally take over, he answered, 'I don't believe the day will come when they will kill me. I am prepared and I want to stay here. I mean they could lock me up maybe, but I don't think they will kill me. Even the Gang of Four weren't killed.' No, but two died in prison, Chiang Ching committed suicide while under house arrest, and the fourth lingers on . . . in prison.

THE CASE FOR ELECTIONS

Unless you can change a government by peaceful means, such as periodic elections, then there's bound to be bloodshed. I mean, how do you remove the government when there are no elections. You either kill them, or there is a revolution, or coup d'état, and all these things are unstable. Once in power, people won't give it up unless there is a mechanism for turning them out of office.

Martin Lee

ADRENALIN REPLACES OPIUM

WE WERE UNABLE TO COMPLETE THE HOLIDAY INN. I WENT ACROSS TO THE HONGKONG AND SHANGHAI BANK. AT THAT TIME THINGS WERE DIFFICULT IN HONG KONG . . . THE CHAIRMAN WAS MICHAEL SANDBERG. I WAS LOOKING FOR MONEY. HE SAID, 'WHAT HAVE YOU GOT?' I SAID, 'I HAVE NOTHING, ALL MY THINGS ARE MORTGAGED.' HE SAID, 'WHAT ABOUT YOUR HOUSE?' . . . THAT I WILL NEVER MORTGAGE, NO MATTER WHAT HAPPENS. THAT BELONGS TO MY FAMILY. I WOULD NEVER RISK IT. NEVER . . . I WAS DESPERATE. BUT HE SAID, 'THERE IS SOMETHING ELSE YOU CAN GIVE ME.' I SAID, 'ANYTHING, JUST ASK.' HE SAID, 'YOU CAN GIVE ME YOUR WORD, YOUR SIGNATURE.' ON THAT BASIS HE LENT ME THE MONEY TO FINISH THE HOTEL. WITHOUT IT I WOULD HAVE BEEN RUINED . . .

Hari Harilela

One of the great figures of Hong Kong's early history was William Jardine, known to the Chinese community as 'The Iron-headed Rat'. The only chair in his office was his own; those who came to do business with him were forced to stand; it shortened interviews. Jardine was born at Lochmaben, Scotland, in 1784, and joined the East India Company as a ship's surgeon in 1802, when he was eighteen. In 1819, he left the comfortable embrace of the Company to enter business, as an agent for the firm of Framjee Cowasjee, owned by Parsee Indians from Bombay. The Parsees are a close-knit religious

子曰道千乘之國
敬事而信節用而
愛人使民以時

In guiding a state of
a thousand chariots,
approach your duties with
seriousness of purpose and
sincerity, love those
around you, be prudent
and employ only those
necessary to complete
the work at hand.

community practising Zoroastrianism; they have achieved a widespread economic success far outweighing their numbers. The Scots are not a closely knit community, but when they practice business, they, too, seem to produce over-achievers. Jardine was one of these.

With another Scot, James Matheson, he founded the Princely Hong in 1832, a company that continues, under the name of Jardine & Matheson, to be a major force in Hong Kong today. Jardine and Matheson were typical of the colony's early entrepreneurs – staunchly white, sturdily British, proudly prejudiced, incurably optimistic and almost off-handedly crooked. They worked hard, risked mightily, and ran roughshod over any local laws that stood in the way of profit. In the early years, they traded almost exclusively in opium, buying in India and smuggling the drug into the myriad coves and harbours of the Fukien coast, to sell to distributors there. A chest of Bengal opium could reach as much as $1,375, and by the late 1830s, Jardine & Matheson were handling 6,000 chests a year, and making what was then the staggering annual profit of $100,000. When the Chinese attempted to interfere with this trade, as we have seen, the result was two Opium Wars, fought by the British on behalf of the traders, and ending with the almost complete capitulation of China, and the establishment of huge fortunes in Hong Kong.

Even in the age of the Robber Barons, the Iron-headed Rat stood out, but most of the early entrepreneurs shared common characteristics. They worked hard, played hard, stuck to their own kind, and were willing to undertake enormous gambles, following their own instincts. True, they tried to ensure the outcome, by working with their rivals to squeeze down the prices they paid for goods, and by pressuring their own government to impose favourable treaties on the Chinese, but they were gamblers, every one, and many of them went to the wall.

The entrepreneurs of today in Hong Kong share only a few of these characteristics. Very few of them are white, and racial prejudice is neither acceptable nor affordable; some are staunchly British, but most could be called staunchly adaptable, instead; and, most of them, most of the time, play by the rules, both because it makes sense to do so, and because, in modern Hong Kong, the worth of a business-person's word, as we see in the quotation at the top of this chapter, is a negotiable commodity.

Where the nineteenth-century buccaneers and the modern entrepreneurs come together is in hard work, self-confidence, ingenuity, optimism and willingness to take appalling risks for enormous profit. Consider the case of the Kadoories, a family with widespread interests and a vivid history.

THE KADOORIES

It was to be his last interview. He died seven months later, in August 1993, three months before Snowdon was to take his portrait. In December 1992, *The South China Morning Post* carried the announcement of Lord Kadoorie's retirement as Chairman of China Light & Power. He was ninety-three at the time. His only son, Michael, then fifty-two, assumed control of the Kadoorie family interests, which include the Peninsula Hotel, the Hongkong and Shanghai Hotels Ltd, and Hong Kong Carpet. Lord Kadoorie's brother, Sir Horace Kadoorie, renowned for his many and varied philanthropic interests, died in April 1995, aged ninety-three.

No. 2 Ice House Street, Central, is an address that is beautiful for being so elemental and unusual. It speaks of a time before technology, and of a location with purpose. It avoids the typical colonial references to monarchy, forgotten taipans or long-dead governors. It certainly suits the Kadoorie family. They named their famous hotel the 'Peninsula', not the 'Royal' this nor the 'Imperial' that, they named it from where it rose, on the Kowloon Peninsula.

Ms Weir, a no-nonsense middle-aged Englishwoman, led us into Lord Kadoorie's large, dark-panelled office. It was clear she had been his secretary for many years. When she interrupted our interview an hour or so later, Lord Kadoorie referred to her as his policewoman, assigned to keep him out of trouble.

He was elegant, articulate, gracious and charming. But old-world charm hid an iron will.

After greeting us warmly, he led us to a conference table in one corner of his office. A large photograph of his father, Sir Elly Kadoorie, dominated one wall. Lord Kadoorie stood at the head of the table and motioned us to sit at either side. The more experienced or wary subjects run their own tape recorders during interviews. Ms Weir made sure Lord Kadoorie's was well placed and in working order before taking her leave. Lord Kadoorie was experiencing some discomfort from a pinched nerve in his neck, otherwise he appeared a good fifteen years younger than his age. And though it was a month since his official retirement, he was still working an eight-hour day.

He was a short, compactly built man. His eyes were clear and quick and his hearing sharp. He wore a dark blue, beautifully tailored pin-stripe suit with a white handkerchief carefully arranged in his breast pocket. His most striking feature was his large, elegant hands. He lay them out on the table in front of him and occasionally used them to emphasize a point with careful, economic gestures. And his fingernails were beautifully manicured, startling for a man who spoke with such relish of the physical price of hard labour, of working himself to exhaustion and loving every minute. He recalled the grinding work of rebuilding Hong Kong after the devastation of World War II:

> It was hard work, but enjoyable work. I mean, if you loved it, you loved it! But for me I would work till 3 o'clock in the morning – fell asleep in the chair, almost. But it didn't matter, you felt you were doing something.

Elly Kadoorie arrived in Hong Kong via Bombay on 20 May 1880. He was hired by E. D. Sassoon and Company as a clerk at thirty-seven rupees a month, and fired after an incident in Ningpo. There had been an outbreak of plague and Elly had withdrawn a barrel of disinfectant from the stores without the permission of senior management. He returned to Hong Kong and set himself up as a broker with Sassoon Benjamin and George Potts. The firm took the name Benjamin, Kelly (derived from Elly) and Potts. One of the local companies they promoted was China Light & Power, then under the direction of Robert Shewan. A close friendship soon developed between Robert Shewan and Sir Elly that would eventually lead to Kadoorie's investment in China Light.

Sir Elly met the Sephardi philanthropist Frederick Mocatta during a trip to England in the late 1890s and married his niece, Laura Mocatta, in 1897. The Mocatta family had fled from Spain to Holland at the time of the Inquisition. They had later settled in England and in 1684 established the firm Mocatta and Goldsmid, who have been bullion brokers to the Bank of England since 1696. Thus, the union in marriage of the two families reinforced a mutual, native capacity for business, and resulted in the birth of two children who would inherit the talent.

Lawrence Kadoorie was born in Hong Kong in 1899, his brother Horace in London in 1902. The family was wealthy now, and retired to England in 1910, where the two boys were at school. But a series of events brought them back to the East, to Hong Kong, and to a far vaster fortune. The first step came in 1911, when Sir Elly's business began to suffer from his absence, and he returned to Asia, to Shanghai, to set things straight again. That process was well under way when, in 1914, the Kadoories were vacationing in Canada and World War I broke out. They were forced to remain there, cut off from funds, until their money was finally exhausted. And eventually made their way back to Shanghai, where they remained for the duration of the war:

57

There never was and never will be another city like Shanghai between the two wars – a city of extreme contrasts, combining the attributes of East and West. The Paris of the Orient . . . a paradise for adventurers. Here my brother and I continued our education – the international outlook of Shanghai broadening ours and giving us an understanding of what it was to become a citizen of the world.

The family acquired the St George's Building in the early 1920s. We were interviewing Lord Kadoorie in the penthouse of the new St George's Building in January 1993. Lord Kadoorie recalled the circumstances of the acquisition:

One Saturday afternoon in London, it was pouring with rain, a horrible day. The front door bell rang, and who should be outside in a very wet raincoat but Robert Shewan. He said, 'Oh, Kadoorie, I was passing and came in. Can you help me out? Can you let me have some cash? It's Saturday, and I can't cash a cheque and I'm stuck.'

Shewan was invited in for tea. During the course of their conversation, he told Sir Elly that he'd been offered the St George's Building, one of Hong Kong's finest. Sir Elly suggested they join that interest with some of Sir Elly's businesses, as well as a piece of land he owned in Kowloon. Shortly after setting up their new company the Hong Kong real estate market collapsed and Sir Elly was forced to assume Shewan's interests, including the St George's Building. It was also in the 1920s that Sir Elly built the family's residence in Shanghai, Marble Hall.

The Kadoories moved into the hotel business at this same time. Sir Elias Kadoorie, Sir Elly's brother, had established a holding firm, The Hongkong and Shanghai Hotels Ltd, and when he died in 1922, this company was taken over by Sir Elly and his two sons, Lawrence, later Lord Kadoorie, and Horace, now Sir Horace. That same year, they began construction of their masterpiece, the Peninsula Hotel. It was a long, expensive struggle. First, to overcome the problems caused by excessive ground water, it was necessary to drive 600 piles deep into the earth. Then, there was the labour unrest that culminated in the general strike of 1925. Finally, British military forces, transferred to the colony because of worsening conditions in China's ongoing civil war, took over the still-incomplete hotel for several months in 1927. It was not until 11 December 1928, that the Peninsula opened her doors to the general public, and immediately began to do brisk business.

However, the real upward thrust in the family fortunes came, not from real estate, or hotels, but from the giant electric company, China Light & Power, and involved the same Robert Shewan who had led them to the St George's building.

Robert Gordon Shewan was a founding partner in the firm of Shewan, Tomes & Company, and Managing Director of Russel and Company of Hong Kong. He was to become Chairman of Green Island Cement Company and sit on the boards of the Hongkong and Shanghai Banking Corporation and *The South China Morning Post*. He was also the elected representative on the Legislative Council for the Hong Kong Chamber of Commerce. On 23 April 1900, Shewan's company registered The China Light & Power Syndicate Ltd. The Hongkong Electric Company had been supplying Hong Kong Island with

I DREAMT I DWELT . . .

Unfortunately, the architect, a certain Mr Graham Brown, a stepson of the famous actress Marie Tempest, took to drink, with the result that this residence became a palace. To put it mildly, it was something of a surprise to us, upon our return to Shanghai, to find the architect in hospital with the DTs, and a house with a ballroom 65 feet high, 80 feet long and 50 feet wide, and a verandah 225 feet long.

Happily my father was fond of entertaining friends, and Marble Hall became well known to visitors from all parts of the world . . . I went back once (after 1949). It's quite well kept. And it's quite a place to go and see. If you ever go to Shanghai, go and see it . . .

Lord Kadoorie

electricity since 1890. Shewan's intention was to create a company to provide power to the recently ceded area of the New Territories. Several months after its founding, China Light & Power absorbed the Canton Electric & Fire Extinguishing Company, founded by Fung Wa-chuen in 1898 to provide power to Canton.

Fung Wa-chuen, a native Chinese, was the first to bring commercial electricity to China; he was a comprador of Russel and Company, Shewan's firm, so it made sense to join the firms.

In 1901, the company was reorganized under the name of the China Light & Power Company Ltd. Fire was the great fear in Chinese villages where streets were narrow and living quarters close and cramped. As Robert Shewan argued, 'In consequence of the fear of fire which very naturally haunts the minds of the shopkeepers, the electric light is growing in popularity every day. To such people as the proprietors of theatres, restaurants, flower boats [floating brothels], and to all those indoors, the advantage of our light over kerosene is obvious.'

Despite this advantage, the early years were very difficult for China Light. The Canton operation continued to lose money, and it was difficult to maintain coal supplies and spare parts for turbines and boilers. Shewan pushed the company forward but by 1911, when the Kowloon population was estimated to be close to 68,000, only 500 were registered customers.

For the next seventeen years, the company struggled on, slowly expanding, until, in 1928, the sudden death of Lee Hysan, a major shareholder, brought on a crisis. To pay his death duties, his heirs were forced to sell their shares in the firm, and Shewan turned to his friend Sir Elly Kadoorie, to buy these. He did, joining the board of China Light & Power in 1929. His son, Lawrence, became a board member the next year, and in 1935, became Chairman of the board, the position he held for thirty-seven years, relinquishing it only a month before our interview.

Under the Kadoories, China Light & Power became a dynamic, fast-growing and efficient company, and today remains one of the key firms in Hong Kong, and beyond. One of Lord Kadoorie's proudest achievements was to supervise the construction of the firm's Daya Bay nuclear-powered electrical generation facility in mainland China.

59

Sir Elly was in Hong Kong at the time of the Japanese invasion in December 1941. He had moved down to Hong Kong to avoid Shanghai's cold winters. The Japanese interned the family at Stanley Camp. As Lord Kadoorie remembered:

> *The Japanese, knowing that he had done so much for education in this part of the world, and trying at that time to press forward their co-prosperity sphere idea, seemed to think that it was a good idea to get rid of him . . . They approached me in the camp. They proposed a scheme to get the family up to Shanghai. They decided to make me a Canadian newspaper man. I don't mind being Canadian, but I'd rather not have been a newspaperman. Anyway, they told me I could buy tickets to Shanghai on a small boat . . . So we got on to a ship called* Taiwan Maru – *a very small ship – together with members of the Consular Corps. There were two thousand people on this ship. The Japanese had life-belts, no one else had. We were packed solid. It took nine days to get to Shanghai and we weren't allowed on deck except in the evening. We went to Taiwan but they didn't allow us off. We managed to get a little fruit . . . So we went to Shanghai, to find our house had been taken by the Japanese.*

Lord Kadoorie returned to Hong Kong at the end of the war on the first British plane out of Shanghai:

> *Hong Kong was a very different place from what I had left . . . First of all, there were rats everywhere. Eighteen inches long! We were scared of them . . . I remember going to the Peninsula Hotel, which had been taken over by the military. After making a big fuss and saying I was the Chairman, at last I got a room there. I had a cup of tea with two lumps of*

sugar in the saucer. The phone rang. I went to the telephone and when I returned my two lumps of sugar had disappeared. The rats had eaten them.

The Japanese military had occupied the Peninsula Hotel during the war. The hotel had survived aerial bombardment but was threatened by damage done in the last days of its occupation:

The Japanese had poured caustic soda down the lavatories. The result was that the pipes, the cast-iron pipes, had become as soft as butter. You could push your finger in and make a hole. Unfortunately, the pipes are all buried in the walls and they're leaking everywhere. So a big decision had to be taken. The cheapest way, the most practical way, would have been to tear down the hotel. To demolish. That would have been the cheapest. But if we'd done that we would have lost our staff. They would have gone elsewhere during the rebuilding and we'd never get them back. It's your staff that makes you a success and we didn't want to lose them. So what we did is . . . we cut the hotel into sections like a cake, opened it up one section at a time, did the repairs and then moved to the next section. That's how we kept our staff and kept the hotel in operation . . .

He had told these stories many times before. Like all great storytellers he was constantly attending to his audience – fixing our eyes with his, raising his elegant hands to underline an important point, or shrugging slightly in resignation. His memories were so very alive and clear to us because he delivered them with the feeling he had had at the time they occurred.

When he talked about the period of reconstruction after the war, we could feel his regret at a time of innocence past, and the memory of the excitement of those adrenalin-charged days.

It was a great period in Hong Kong. Everyone worked so hard . . . It was wonderful, you'd work until 3am and fall into bed exhausted . . . But it didn't last. I remember when it ended. You see there were few cars, no transport, and anyone who had a car would stop to give someone on the street a lift. I knew it had all come to an end when one day I stopped to offer a woman a lift and she just stared at me as if I were mad. She refused the offer. I knew then that we were moving into another time . . .

We pressed him about the years of reconstruction after the war. The flood of wealthy Shanghai entrepreneurs fleeing Mao's China, the developing Cold War and tensions in Korea and Vietnam, and hundreds of thousands of ordinary refugees adding to the pool of cheap labour:

Hong Kong itself was like a snowball. As it moved along, it gathered momentum, bigger, bigger and bigger, until . . . You see what it is like today. Well today we are passing through somewhat difficult times. But personally I remain optimistic. I believe there is a big future for this part of the world, and I think Hong Kong is destined to play a very important part in that future . . .

It was very moving to see a man of such age and experience still looking at the future with optimism. He was alive and engaged in the moment. He understood the nature of the human experience, and the profound impression one being can make on another:

. . . When you go away, you'll be different when you go out this door than from when you came in . . . And I will be different from when you came in . . .

It was nearing the end of our time with him. It was past five in the afternoon, but he showed neither fatigue nor loss of enthusiasm for the subject matter or for his guests. When he'd finally decided he'd had enough, he pushed a hidden button at the end of the table where he sat and within seconds Ms Weir was at the door.

As we rose to leave he directed us to the astonishing collection of carved ivory and jade in the glass cabinet lining one wall of his office. He pointed out pieces of particular interest to him. They were never the most elaborate or ostentatious, but they were objects with great stories about their creation or acquisition.

Finally, as we were about to leave, he pulled open a drawer and lifted out a small glass bottle that had melted and collapsed in on itself. He handed it to us. He asked us what we though of it. It was old and melted. There was nothing to say. 'Hiroshima,' he said quietly. 'It was picked up off the ground at Hiroshima . . . I keep it to remind me . . .' He took it back. He held it in one hand and examined it. After a moment of silence he looked up at us and smiled, shrugged, and replaced it, closing the drawer quietly.

He walked us to the lift, waited for us to enter, then bowed slightly in that old-world way, and wished us well.

We corresponded with Lord Kadoorie over the next few months. By early summer he was using a wheelchair. The last letter we received from him came in late July; his signature was weak, unsure, fading.

Lord Kadoorie died in August 1993. Vincent Lo told us that he had attended a meeting in Lord Kadoorie's office a week or so before his death. He said that Lord Kadoorie was clearly frail and failing and now confined to a wheelchair. He said that it was a meeting that lasted several hours, and included a number of very powerful individuals. At the end of the meeting, after the group had reached consensus, Lord Kadoorie called in Ms Weir and dictated a letter summarizing the group's position. Lord Kadoorie dictated the letter in front of them: it came out of his mouth faultless and fully formed and summarized the long discussion and conclusion impeccably. Lo said it was astonishing to see the power of such a mind, and such will, in so frail a man.

We arrived in Hong Kong with Lord Snowdon a few months after Lord Kadoorie's death. During our visit, we attended the opening of an international art fair held in the Hong Kong Convention Centre. Great paintings and sculpture from the world's foremost dealers were being offered up to the Hong Kong market. *Everyone* was there. Lord Snowdon ran into Lord Litchfield, the Queen's cousin, and a noted photographer also on assignment in Hong Kong. And we met Lord Kadoorie's children, Michael and Rita. We told Rita how her father epitomized for us the spirit of Hong Kong's entrepreneurs, the eternal optimism, the gambler's nerve and the opportunist's instincts. She has her father's clear brown eyes and much the same smile.

It was an evening of powerful images and resonating memories. As we took the escalator down to the ground floor, we looked out across the harbour and saw Lord Kadoorie's Peninsula Hotel. It had defined the Kowloon Peninsula for many years, but now was much diminished by surrounding towers. Then we saw the construction cranes: tall black silhouettes in the night sky. A newer, greater Peninsula was in the works, and before our book would be finished the Peninsula would once again be the centre and focus of Kowloon-side Hong Kong.

GOOD FENG SHUI

I was born in a house in Robinson Road. And this house had a garden. My father liked gardens very much. Now, in those days if you bought land there was a condition, you had to build on the land within a certain time. But they didn't say how big you had to build. You could build a small thing or big, it didn't matter so long as you built. So my father applied for a large piece of land and he built six tennis courts with a little pavilion in the middle, and that was it. So the government came along and said, 'When are you going to build?' 'I built here, can't you see it?' They said they had since changed the law, and they now said you had to build according to the size of the land you had. At the time our house was built against the hill. And one day all the servants came and said, 'You can't stay here any more. Terrible bad *feng shui*. There are awful screams of somebody being killed.' Sure enough we went outside and there were horrible screams coming from the hill behind the house. We had no idea what was going on. And then a peacock flew out from the garden next door. It was these peacocks making all the noise. Once we discovered what it was all about the good *feng shui* returned and all went well after that.

Lord Kadoorie

THE HARILELAS

We did our best to have all six Harilela brothers in Hong Kong at the same time. Though the family lives, literally, under one roof at 1 Durham Road, Kowloon, their business empire spans the globe, and keeps most of them travelling six months out of twelve.

Bob, born in 1930, is missing from the portrait, as is a young sister, Sandee, born in 1947. Another sister, Rani (1936), died in June 1992. But culturally, or philosophically, it is the Harilela brothers who have created the empire and the legend.

Lord Snowdon was not concerned. He said that it was extremely difficult to compose a single portrait of six people; an odd number offers a better balance. But he went further still and separated the five brothers into two groupings. He has the older three, Hari (1922), Peter (1926) and George (1920), the eldest, on page 63, and the youngest brothers, Gary (1934) and Michael (1945) on page 65.

Though George is the eldest, it is Hari who is the entrepreneur of vision, and the family's driving force. But there are still matters in which deference is shown to the eldest.

We told the brothers that Lord Snowdon wanted them in something other than their standard dark suit, white shirt and tie. They never actually said no to the change, but nor did they offer suggestions of other attire. We asked them if they had any traditional Indian clothes. They said they would never be photographed in such things. Except for George, who loved the idea.

The brothers arrived separately, and at different times, from business meetings and locations throughout the colony. As their number grew, it seemed more like a gathering of company directors waiting for a quorum, than subjects for a sitting. As soon as they saw one another they would begin discussing the business they had just left. They settled in a quiet corner and talked in hushed tones. It all seemed very serious and secret. George was the last to arrive, and just in time, as the others had finished their conference and seemed impatient to be back at work.

The limousine seemed jammed with bodies and bundles. George tumbled out of the door. He was beaming. This was his conspiracy. A parade of granddaughters followed, each carrying an armful of festive Indian robes.

George entered the studio. His four younger brothers were talking quietly in a circle. They looked up and smiled. When the costume-carrying granddaughters filed by, they paled. They

instinctively turned to Hari for support or guidance. The clothes went into an adjacent room. George approached the tightening circle of siblings. He moved in among them. Hari was steely-eyed and determined. He kept shaking his head, no. We felt it best to leave them alone, and George to his fate.

It took longer to change clothes than it had taken to change their minds. George was beaming and renewed. He has an attic full of these robes, which he wears to celebrate Indian holidays and to honour the culture and customs of his native land. George is a big, gentle man. He speaks softly, and whispers if it is something he thinks is important. His manner is solicitous but always sincere. It took some time to summon the courage to question him about what is perhaps his most striking feature: a row of hair grows up the outer edge of each ear. These grey angel-like wings extend two inches. He waxes them carefully to keep them in place. He told us that such hair is a sign of good fortune. He's very proud of it, and not in the least shy about discussing such pious ostentation. We only regret that such a feature, and such a wise and gentle face, could not be given the prominence it deserves.

There are approximately eighty thousand people of Indian descent in Hong Kong. The Harilelas are the first family of this community. It is a community comprised of Moslems, Hindus, Sikhs and Christians from India, Pakistan, Malaysia, Indonesia and the Middle East. The Harilelas are Sindhis from Hyderabad.

The first Harilela fortune was lost when the boys were very young. It is perhaps the pain of watching their father suffer such humiliation that has made them so very determined to succeed. And their passionate and detailed descriptions of the family's diverse holdings suggest that they will never be extensive enough, nor the fortune vast enough, to allay the nagging insecurity that is the scar of such boyhood trauma.

In 1922 Lilaram Harilela moved his wife and sons, George and Hari, from India to Shanghai. He later moved to Guangzhou where the family began to enjoy the fruits of Lilaram's success. Hari remembers the big house and large sampan the family would relax on each weekend. The company was called the Daru Star, and sold jade, amber and oriental arts. The stock market crash of 1929 brought an end to the business. Hari explained that much of his father's business was with American importers who worked on thirty, sixty or ninety day lines of credit. The crash wiped out most of his American clients, and dried up the flow of capital he needed to pay off his Chinese suppliers. The family moved from Guangzhou to Hong Kong in December 1929.

The 1930s were difficult years as the Harilelas struggled to rebuild their fortune. The boys were sent out to work as soon as they were able. Hari sold newspapers on the street; Lilaram found work for George, selling to tourists.

Lilaram spoke sixteen languages and finally found work as a census officer. Eventually, the family saved enough money to open a small shop. The boys scoured the city looking for merchandise, while their mother tended the store.

The Japanese occupation of 1941 brought an end to business. Lilaram's work as a census officer almost cost him his life. Late one night, Japanese soldiers broke down the door of the family's home and took their parents away. George approached an officer on horseback and pleaded with him to have his parents released. Miraculously, two hours later the officer returned with the elder Harilelas. Lilaram had been badly beaten. The officer explained that they had probably been arrested because they hadn't answered the door promptly, and the patrolling soldiers had over-reacted.

During the occupation, the boys bought and sold what they could to survive. Hari made dawn-to-dusk excursions to sell rice in restricted areas. He was often caught out after curfew and severely beaten.

British forces occupied Hong Kong after the war. Supplies were still limited. The boys stumbled upon some old sewing machines, and found space in Tsim Sha Tsui opposite the Peninsula Hotel where they opened a small shop. British soldiers in need of tailoring were their first customers. They often traded work for food or other supplies the British might have. Their reputation began to grow and they eventually won a contract to supply the British with ten thousand uniforms. George explained how the military came to depend on them:

> *They came to know us. Every day they came to us and said we need this, or we need that. But we didn't know where to go. They said, 'You speak good Chinese, find it for us. We need vegetables, eggs, fresh meat.' I said we need trucks. Hari took the truck. I looked after the shop, Peter looked after the sales and I took care of the money. That's how it all started. Hari would go to the farms in the New Territories, talk to the farmers, and buy from them to sell to the armed forces . . . The business was very good.*

The family soon won exclusive contracts to supply the British Army. By the 1950s, they owned thirty-two shops in Kowloon and Hong Kong. By the late fifties their businesses were turning out six hundred suits a day.

The American military used Hong Kong for R&R during the Korean and Vietnam Wars. They discovered the Harilelas shops where a suit could be measured, cut, sewn, fitted and delivered in less than eight hours.

65

They couldn't believe it. They sent TV crews. They filmed it all . . . We measured the customer and told them to come back for the fitting in two hours. Then four hours later come and see the lining. Eight hours and it's done . . . They say this on American TV. It was shown all over America.

It was Hari's idea to move into the property market in the 1960s. They would buy a property and hold onto it only long enough to make a reasonable profit. Hari explained:

Real estate started slowly . . . As Hong Kong grew, as more people came, especially to this area [Kowloon], we did very well. Sometimes within weeks of paying the deposit on a building someone would jump up and double the price. That's how it happened . . . Then we moved into the hotel business.

The Hong Kong government began to encourage the construction of hotels in the mid-1960s in the hope that more tourists would visit the colony.

I went into the hotel business by accident. There was a Chinese group, three partners who wanted to put up a hotel. It is now called the Imperial Hotel . . . I needed more space for a bigger store. I invested in the hotel so I could get the basement and ground floor for my stores . . . Well, the three partners started fighting and one came to me and said, 'We can't finish the hotel, do you want to take it over?' I didn't want it. I didn't know anything about hotels but I took it on. Anyway, that's how we got into the hotel business.

Hari's proudest achievement is the 650-room Holiday Inn Golden Mile in Kowloon. He bought the land just before the troubles of 1967–8, but construction was not complete until 1975.

Our mother passed away on the very day the hotel was to open. It was the saddest day in my life . . . Of course we couldn't participate in the opening. We sent my little son to open the hotel. A lot of people said to cancel the opening but the show must go on. That's the way we feel we should run our business.

On one side of the white card is a standard invitation with blank spaces for the guest's name, the occasion, and the date and time, which are written in by hand. The other side bears a photograph of the Harilela palace in Kowloon Tong. The 22,500-square-foot residence is surrounded by a twelve-foot wall topped with ferocious-looking barbed wire. Access to the compound is through two solid-steel gates. The six Harilela brothers, their sister, their wives and some of their children live under this one roof. In addition to forty-one family members, there are twenty-two maids, six drivers, four security guards, three cooks, two electricians, a manager and a full-time tailor.

The original home was built in 1953, but had only eighteen bedrooms. Hari had this house built in 1968 to accommodate the extended and ever-extending family. He eventually added an annexe containing eight self-contained 2,600 square-foot flats. The two adjoining residences have a total of seventy bedrooms. The garage under the main house can accommodate thirty cars, including four Rolls-Royces; the garage under the annexe can hold another twenty-two vehicles.

The gates had been left open for us. When the limousine pulled up, the guards rose from their comfortable chairs and the house manager, Andrew De Costa, stepped forward to open the car door. The family had been alerted, and very quickly a few of the Harilela brothers, and dozens of small grandchildren, began pouring out of the front door to greet us.

Every Sunday the Harilelas gather the family together for dinner with any friends who happen to be in town. There are three dining rooms with adjoining salons for pre-dinner drinks and conversation, or after-dinner cigars and cognac. The dining room the family uses most frequently has a table made of a huge single piece of glass. The underside is decorated with an acid-etched floral motif. The table can seat eighteen people comfortably. The adjoining dining room, just off the kitchen, is where the grandchildren eat. It has an equally impressive wood table of similar dimensions. But we were to eat in the Moghul Room, the formal dining room at the other end of the house, with two round glass tables capable of seating a total of seventy-two.

Introductions were interminable, as all the tiny nieces and nephews, and children, grandchildren and great-grandchildren had to be properly presented.

Hari insisted that Lord Snowdon had dined at the house on an earlier occasion. Snowdon was polite but firm in saying he hadn't. If he had, he wouldn't have forgotten. How could anyone possibly forget such an experience?

On our way to the dining room, we made a side trip to the roof. There are no lifts: Hari believes that the endless staircase winding up the inside of the three-storey building is good for body and soul.

The roof is flat and separated into areas for play or repose. We can see all of Kowloon, and the lights of Hong Kong across the bay. George's grandson, Sanjay, explains that the annexe next door was constructed to provide the newer generations with both space and freedom. Some would have preferred to move away entirely, but Hari likes to keep the family close. This is the compromise. Sanjay describes conflicts and tensions in the family that older generations might never admit to. For the older generations, to speak of something is to make it real. Silence is the best defence, but a defence that only puts off the inevitable. Suddenly, from out of the sky behind him appears the exposed belly of a 747 jumbo jet on final descent to Kai Tak Airport. Sanjay's lips move, he does not flinch, we do not hear a word he is saying. The plane seems about to scrape us off the roof; we can read the trademark on the tyres. It presses the air down onto us in a hot thick blanket and then is gone. 'You get used to it. After a while you don't even notice it any more,' explains Sanjay. Shaken, we descend to dinner.

The meal is a mixture of Indian and Chinese delicacies, and course after course is offered until we can eat no more. Lord Snowdon is exhausted from his flight from London, but is faultlessly charming, witty and relaxed. It is impossible to know what he really thinks or feels of this Kowloon baptism. We move to an adjacent salon, heavily carpeted and cushioned, and relax with coffee and cognac.

In Hong Kong, it is customary to accompany your guests to the front door and wave them off as their car pulls out into the traffic. There is a formality and finality to the gesture, like waving goodbye to a troop-laden ship sailing off to war. We quickly learned the protocol ourselves and would stand patiently with our guests as their car was brought up to the hotel door, stand quietly as they buckled themselves in, and then smile and wave until the car disappeared.

The Harilelas followed us out to our car. We said our goodbyes and shook all the hands that were offered. The Harilelas waved. We waved back. We waited impatiently for the driver to put the car in gear. Lord Snowdon offered a tip. He suggested we not look at our hosts until the car began to move. The trick is to look up and wave only after the car has begun to move. The grinding of gears, and the meshing of cultures, sent us safely on our way.

TOUGH WORK

My father could have found me a job with a nice person, but no, he wanted to find me a job where I could learn something. This man had a retail store. We sold to tourists. He would go down to the docks and bring the tourists from the boats to the store. I had to sell. Sometimes I would go to the ships and sell to the tourists. I learnt many things from this man. But I tell you, it was very tough, eighteen hours a day. I would tell my mother I am so tired, I'm dying, and my father would give me a slap. 'No, you must do the job that has been given you . . .'

George Harilela

CHIANG CHEN

We conducted the interview at the head office of his manufacturing company in Tai Po, New Territories. Dr Chiang does not speak English, so the interview was conducted in Cantonese with his daughter, Lily, acting as interpreter. Lily is the only one of Dr Chiang's children to follow her father into the business. When we asked him why that was so, and remarked on how unusual it was in Hong Kong to see a daughter taking over such a large business, he explained that she is the only one of his children who can tolerate his temperament. He admits to being impatient and demanding. Lily concurs, and adds that she is much the same.

Chiang Chen was born to a poor family in Shandong, China, in 1923. His early years were extremely difficult and he remembers his family on the brink of starvation, and often with barely enough clothing or blankets to keep them from freezing to death. His mother died when he was two, and his father when he was ten. After his father's death, he set off for Nanking with his older brother Chiang Peng. Chiang was unable to enter school in Nanking because of the poor quality of education he had received in Shandong. As compensation, and to try and bring himself up to a level that would allow him to enter school, he began to read Confucius.

The Sino-Japanese War of 1937 forced the two boys to move once again. Chiang was thirteen when they settled in Chongqing, Sichuan Province. Again he was unable to enter school and went to work as an office boy in a large magazine publishing company. He told us that he was encouraged to read by his fellow workers, doing his best to broaden his horizons. He added popular Kung Fu novels to the steady diet of Confucius.

The Japanese Army was far superior to the Chinese forces, and soon had Chongqing under attack by aerial bombardment. He and his brother fled to the countryside, but the brother was caught and jailed by the Japanese because he had been a government employee. After his release in 1943, the two young men decided to join the pro-Japanese Youth Army. It was a difficult and dangerous decision to make, but the year that he spent being trained by the Japanese

LOVE, HATE AND FEAR

China looks at Hong Kong with love, hate and fear . . . With love because we are Chinese, and because of the contribution Hong Kong makes to China as an international financial centre. With hate because the people of Hong Kong ask for so much. And with fear because China needs Hong Kong and yet may lose it . . . By lose it I mean something might happen that would cause Hong Kong to no longer be an international centre after 1997 . . .
Chiang Chen

changed Chiang's life. The steady diet made him healthy, the education helped him to understand broader, more complex issues, and the military training taught him tactics and strategy.

After Japan's surrender, the Kuomintang found that these young people were all well educated and trained. They didn't want to just tell them to all go home. So they kept us all together and gave us a further year's training. After this additional year, the high command said those that wanted could return home. I liked the training and the army and so I stayed with the Kuomintang forces until the Communist victory in 1949. That's when I came to Hong Kong.

THE STUDENT CHALLENGE

The biggest limitation for students is the political system. After the people finish their studies in Japan or Germany or the United States or Hong Kong, when they go back, their know-how is useless because the government won't utilize them or support them. The reforms could take five to ten years if they go fast, twenty or thirty years if they go slow . . . The longer it takes the more dangerous it is for China. It would allow time for another rebellion or revolution.

Chiang Chen

It is gratitude for these basic lessons, and a belief that these were the tools that made his great success possible, that has led Dr Chiang to establish a foundation that donates money for Chinese scholarships for the advanced education of mainland Chinese.

I've had this idea since I was very young. How can we raise the living standards of the Chinese people? When I was poor, I didn't have the ability to help. Now that I am able to help, I offer all the assistance I can.

Chiang Chen is one of the largest manufacturers of plastic injection-moulding machinery in the world. He explained that he was one of the earliest in the field in the late 1950s. His great innovation came in 1959, when he developed a machine that could make plastic products from two different densities of plastic. No one had been able to develop the technology. The basic problem was the inability of the equipment to handle two different densities of material. He got the idea for the invention from a river in China that empties into the sea. He stood watching how the fresh water and salt water wouldn't mix because of their different densities. At that time injection-moulding for telephones, radios and other household goods was done with great quantities of pre-melted material that was injected by pressure into the mould. The raw material comes in small pellets. If you melted two different densities, or colours, in a large holding vat they would remain separate. Dr Chiang's innovation was to melt the pellets at the point of injection. The different densities had no time to settle or separate.

Dr Chiang sat quietly as Lily translated. He showed no emotion when recounting the difficulties of his youth, or the excitement of his invention. And when we complimented him on his daughter's achievement and the inspiration he must have been for her, he thanked us politely, but impassively, as if we had said we liked the colour of his tie. He did, however, get excited when we questioned him on the environment:

If you break down the normal person's garbage you have approximately thirteen pounds of plastic and fifty-five pounds of paper. Paper is a bigger problem. It takes four hundred years for a city telephone book to degrade and with ink and chemicals it is much more toxic than plastic . . . And we are using less and less plastic in our daily lives, thinner bottles and stronger materials. And ninety-

JEALOUSY

Those who are in power know of the importance of Hong Kong. The general public do not understand. People are jealous of Hong Kong, and this is partly the doing of people in power. They do not want people to long for the Hong Kong way of life. They don't want it to appear to the people that the Communist Party, which is the supreme organization, should be dependent on Hong Kong. So they sometimes tell their people that there are instances of corruption in Hong Kong. They try to debase Hong Kong in their ideology, but this is a political tactic. They themselves are aware of the importance of Hong Kong.

Chiang Chen

eight per cent of it is recycled. A telephone will last a very long time. A fax machine can last a very long time. Your computer and printer, a long time . . . Now, how much paper will you generate with those machines?

He had been sipping tea and warming his hands off the cup. He replaced the lid and put the cup back down on the table as soon as he was finished.

Paper is the big killer in our lives. And they are cutting down too many trees. Blame the paper people . . . Think of all the disposable baby diapers . . . It's the US that wastes the most.

He is confident of Hong Kong's future and the future of his company with his daughter at the helm. As he said, 'If she is no good, the directors will remove her, it has nothing to do with me.'

We thought of Chiang Chen as we drove back to our hotel past Sha Tin racetrack and the forests of high rises that are filling the New Territories. We thought of him looking down at the river in China that emptied into the sea, and wondered what trick might smooth the converging densities of 1997.

FREEDOM, NOT DEMOCRACY

China needs Hong Kong, the finance, the people, the management and communications. And Hong Kong needs China's market . . . What has made Hong Kong? Democracy? No . . . Hong Kong has freedom, but no democracy . . .

Chiang Chen

VINCENT LO

When he walks into the boardroom we look up, but do not stand to greet him. He is in his mid-forties, but looks thirty-five, and is boyishly, and strikingly, handsome. He smiles and introduces himself in a way that suggests that he has been mistaken for a junior assistant before.

Vincent Lo is one of the new generation of Hong Kong entrepreneurs. He is also rare among Chinese billionaires in that he was born and raised in Hong Kong. His father sent him to school in Australia when he was fifteen.

I went on to university to study Economics and returned to Hong Kong in 1969. My family was in the textile business. My father sent me to work at a friend's factory to learn the business. I lasted about six months before I realized that it wasn't the right business for me.

In the early 1970s the property market began to heat up, and the family decided that Vincent might do better in their property business.

It was a very typical family business: my eldest sister, my brothers, everybody was working there. I wasn't very comfortable there because I was the youngest. I could not make many decisions on my own. After eighteen months, I found a job outside the family firm. But my mother wouldn't let me work for somebody else. She said, 'You work for your father or you work for yourself.'

However, his mother pushed his father into lending Vincent US $100,000. He started a construction company, Shui On, because it was something that was related to the family's other holdings, and something his father could advise him on. In fact, his father gave him his first three construction jobs. He then moved into construction materials and invested in properties together with his family. By the early 1980s he had control of the company and had listed it on the Stock Exchange. Shui On remained a public company until 1990, when Lo again privatized it.

GOING SLOW

I'm regarded as a conservative in Hong Kong because I feel we have to take a step by step approach to democracy. It doesn't mean that I don't support democracy or accept democracy. It's just that I see us doing it on a step by step basis. I'm a pragmatic, realistic businessman, not an idealist. I don't believe we can say to the people of Hong Kong that we can just take over the government tomorrow. I just don't believe in that.

Vincent Lo

The reason for making it private was that since 1985 I was very actively involved in drafting the Basic Law. I was an Executive Committee member of the Basic Law Consultative Committee. I was spending a lot of time on the committee, and of course everyone was trying to put the microscope to me and my life. It was made more difficult by being the Chairman and major shareholder of a public company.

BUSINESS VERSUS POLITICS

Personally I prefer business. It's much simpler. You are driven by the profit margin. You negotiate with your associates, with your clients, or whatever, it's clearly driven by the profit margin, and simpler to approach. Whereas in politics . . . I cannot see myself playing the same political games as some of the people are doing now. And I really believe they are screwing up Hong Kong by politicizing the community and advocating the confrontational type of politics so prevalent in the Western democracies.

PROSPERITY IS THE KEY

Economic prosperity is the key to our future. We must maintain that. We have to ask ourselves, why will China accept 'One country, two systems'? What is so special about six million people that makes them give us this special treatment? Because we are useful to China. We're useful to their reforms, we're useful in their economy, and we must maintain that . . . But, apart from our usefulness to China, I don't really see why we should be so special.

Vincent Lo

He took the company private with the help of Henry Cheng, son of Cheng Yu-tung, the founder of New World Development. Cheng held thirty per cent of the company and Lo seventy per cent. 'But last year I bought this thirty per cent share back from them. Now I have one hundred per cent ownership of the company. I find it very relaxing . . .' Besides property and construction materials, Shui On owns a string of hotels. Lo says he is still enjoying the liberty of making decisions without the criticism of shareholders.

Lo is one of the figures whose names are put forward as possible Chief Executive after 1997. But he claims he is moving out of politics and back to business. He has little sympathy for Western-style politics, and suggests that it is a lack of politics that has led to Hong Kong's success, and that politics now threatens its future.

We hardly have any strikes in Hong Kong. But it is going to come, because when it becomes more political then the unionists will try to stir things up, because they will be interested in grabbing more power.

His words seem harder on paper than when he spoke them. His expression was always calm and his emotions in check. He spoke with a slight sense of fatigue, or ennui. The words are bleaker on the page, charged by the impatience of a man who holds real power: economic power.

Lo explains that he has been investing in China for over fifteen years. He has watched the internal changes, the economic reforms, and believes the Chinese understand that they must leave Hong Kong alone, if it is to maintain its prosperity and stability.

He invested in Shanghai and the northern cities, in hotels and property, which proved to be a mistake as their value collapsed after Tiananmen Square.

When we first went in, everything was just very, very bureaucratic. You go to twenty-odd departments to try to get approval . . . Today, they will facilitate your activities. The government is much more pro-business, in the sense that they now understand what business is all about, especially in the southern provinces. They tune into Hong Kong radio and television, they speak the same language, and I don't just mean Cantonese. They actually understand the language of business.

He returns to a discussion of politics. Though he says that he is easing himself out of active politics, and dislikes the game, it is the dynamics of politics and his own very firmly held beliefs that he returns to again and again.

Our concern in the business community is that Hong Kong becomes too socialistic. Of course we would like to provide more for the people who cannot look after themselves, the underprivileged. But if you provide too much of a safety net for everybody, then people will just show up and say, okay, I won't work . . .

The first thing he tells us when we ask him about Beijing politics is that he has come into contact with many of the leaders throughout the years. He is confident that the reforms will continue, that the open door policy and market reforms are irreversible. He is betting on it, and doing whatever he can to retain the environment that allowed his remarkable success.

If we didn't have this sort of environment, I wouldn't be sitting here. I never would be able to own this building, which is worth over HK $4 billion. And I started with just $100,000 twenty years ago. Where else in the world would I find that sort of environment? That's why I feel we must try to maintain this environment. I don't want to be the only one who has benefited from this.

TIMOTHY FOK

Wendy Kwok (Mrs Walter Kwok) introduced us to Tim Fok. They had known each other for years. When we asked about Tim Fok's background and family, Wendy said that today in Hong Kong if you spend money as if there is no tomorrow they say 'Who do you think you are, Li Ka-shing?' In the 1970s, they used to say the same about Tim Fok's father: 'Who do you think you are, Henry Fok?'

Tim Fok's office is in one of the most unusual and beautiful buildings in the world, the I. M. Pei Bank of China building. Its design was inspired by bamboo, which symbolizes growth and prosperity. The angles are fractured and odd, and the inside of the building strangely quiet. It is like being inside a prism as light bounces across grey granite and glazed glass.

When we stepped out of the lift we turned towards the reception and saw the names of a dozen Fok companies listed on the wall. The office is a complete contrast to the cool modernity of I. M. Pei. It is dark wood panelling and shelves; leather-bound books and heavy furniture. It is Victorian and comfortable.

Again, Timothy Fok seems surprisingly young, perhaps thirty-five, but he was born in 1946. However, there is no confusing him for a junior assistant. There is a nervous energy about him, although he is earnest and shy. He is also unusually individualistic. One cannot categorize him by appearance, he is a unique and charming creation. And he is very anxious that we understand Hong Kong, that we do not succumb to cliché:

I hardly fit into the same category as some of the people you have met. At the same time, maybe you want to get the whole spectrum . . . I am not a very important person and I have shied away from any sort of publicity . . . I like to show people the best, take them around, make them at home, and treat them as a friend. I think it's my natural Chinese hospitality. But they get disappointed, because the idea they come with is of a money-grabbing place, with the Chinese eating noodles, while speaking down a mobile phone. But Hong Kong is much more than that.

A CONSTANT REVOLUTION

I think the West suffers from this romanticism. It's the *Washington Post* type of mentality, that one little thing can topple the biggest government. But life here and in China is not like that. Life in China has been a constant revolution for a very long time. It's not one thing that will change it or bring it down; revolution is a constant process.

Timothy Fok

78

Tim Fok was sent to boarding school in 1951 at the age of five; he went to schools in both England and the United States. He started his business career in Vancouver, at the time of the 1967 riots in Hong Kong. He stayed in Vancouver for only one year before deciding that Hong Kong was his real home. It was also the pressure of being the eldest son, and heir to a large family business, that brought him back. Henry Fok, his father, is a legendary business figure, a friend and partner to the casino king Stanley Ho, and one of the first of the big entrepreneurs to invest in China.

Tim Fok believes that one country, two systems is the key to Hong Kong's continued success. He feels that one of the dangers to this approach is the tendency for Western-educated Chinese to constantly question the system. It's not that the system is treating them wrong, it is simply a reflex to question it. He applauds the construction of the airport and any measure that makes Hong Kong more valuable. He adds that Hong Kong and China must begin to integrate their hardware and software, in computers.

WHAT IS DEMOCRACY?

I really don't understand what democracy is. I mean is one man, one vote, democracy? There are many ways to see it. And when you have an election are you really getting the best people? . . . I know who in my company is the best person. I can tell you immediately.

Timothy Fok

Through what channels do we communicate? Our civil service should be going into China and theirs coming here. Many of us here already speak Mandarin.

IT'S NOT ABOUT SHOW

In the West you always judge things by their appearance.

If the man wears an expensive suit and drives a big fancy car he must be

important . . . And in the West, when you build a house, you make the

front of the house the most impressive part. You build big doors and

columns, and tall windows and a big yard out front. All very impressive . . .

The Chinese are different . . . Traditionally, the Chinese house has a very

plain front, a small door, you can't even tell there is a house there. It's

a wall on the street. And when you enter the house, you go through one

small room to the next. Nothing big and fancy. And the most important

room in the house, the central room, where the family meets,

is just like any other room . . . It's not about show. No one

is trying to impress anyone . . .

Timothy Fok

He had to rush, his limousine was waiting to take him to another meeting across town. He accompanied us down in the lift to the ground floor. He hurled himself into the back of his limousine, all the while reminding us of the importance of family and education. The door closed, the window slid open and still he was talking, telling us to call when we were next in town. 'Anytime, call me . . .'

We were at Lord Snowdon's studio in London in June 1994, selecting photographs for this book. The phone rang. Lord Snowdon's secretary came in and said a Mr Timothy Fok had called and was on his way over. We reminded Lord Snowdon who he was. We pulled his picture out from the pile in front of us. 'But, what does he want?' asked Lord Snowdon. Snowdon seemed almost fearful of what lay ahead – as if he were about to be served with legal papers. We reminded him that he had invited Tim Fok to drop by the next time he was in London. Snowdon was just being polite; his invitation had been about form, not content. To Tim Fok, and many Chinese, they are one and the same thing.

79

CORPORATE POWER:

THE QUORUM

I THINK THAT WHATEVER CHANGES THAT MAY TAKE PLACE WILL NOT BE BROUGHT ABOUT BY CHINA. THE QUESTION IS WHETHER HONG KONG PEOPLE ARE FIRM ENOUGH . . . WHY? HONG KONG AT PRESENT IS ALWAYS TALKING ABOUT DEMOCRACY. DEMOCRACY! DO YOU NOT FEEL THAT WHEREVER THERE IS MORE DEMOCRACY, THE ECONOMY WILL BE ON THE DECLINE? IS CANADA NOT IN VERY POOR SHAPE? . . . SOCIAL WELFARE IS MUCH TOO GOOD, SO GOOD THAT PEOPLE HAVE BECOME VERY LAZY. WE DO NOT HAVE SUCH NICE SOCIAL WELFARE IN HONG KONG. WE TALK ABOUT DEMOCRACY IN HONG KONG, TOO. DO WE HAVE DEMOCRACY IN HONG KONG NOW? NO, WE DO NOT. WE ARE RULED BY THE BRITISH GOVERNMENT. I DO NOT UNDERSTAND THE BRITISH GOVERNMENT'S TALK OF DEMOCRACY.

Cheng Yu-tung

Freda said that he had to be photographed at 9am. It was 9am for Peter Woo, or nothing. She was hard and commanding, even angry. It was Lord Snowdon's last full day in Hong Kong and Walter Kwok had asked for the 9am sitting weeks before. Walter does not like interviews or sittings and always puts them off till the very last possible moment. We weren't about to ask Walter to change. The Kwoks had been wonderful hosts. Their hotel had served us perfectly, and the staff had been patient and kind. They had even allowed us to transform the hotel's business centre and boardroom into Snowdon's studio. We wouldn't ask Walter to change his appointment. When we informed Freda that 9am was out of the question, she seemed taken aback. She couldn't imagine us not bending to her will, which, after all,

Tsze-lû asked about government. The Master said, 'Work hard and inspire those around you with your example.' He asked for elaboration and was told, 'Be tenacious.'

represents the will of Peter Woo. But we were exhausted, and time for compromise and pleasantries was short.

She phoned back almost immediately. Gone was the sergeant major's bark. Her voice was light and pleasant. It was a startling transformation, from bully to best friend in the click of a receiver. It was also proof that those in the shadow of the powerful often live their emotional lives vicariously – surfing on the boss's ebb and flow.

Peter Woo arrived at the Royal Garden Hotel on foot, just before 11am. He was the only one of our subjects to arrive by foot. It was his height and confident bearing that made it easy to pick him out of the bustling crowds. He leans forward slightly into the direction he is walking. If he stopped suddenly he might fall. It is impatience and confidence that drive him forward; he strides along as if he could walk through walls.

The doors were held open for him. We greeted and led him to Snowdon's studio. Everything seemed to go very well. Until six months later, when we were back in Hong Kong showing some of the subjects the results of their sittings.

Woo did not like his portrait, but didn't want to say so; he simply stood there, radiating distaste. So did a gaggle of his senior employees, gathered for the unveiling, who managed to convey their silent, supportive displeasure in sympathy with the boss. Woo leafed through the assembled photographs, spread out on a dark, mahogany table. He pointed out the merits of Baroness Dunn's portrait, praising the way Snowdon had captured her confidence, her intelligence, her reserve. He said Joyce Ma's likeness was dignified, elegant and aristocratic. Of his own, he said not a word. Finally, we put him out of his misery; if he didn't like the photograph, the only solution was for him to travel to London for another sitting with Snowdon. And to pay for it himself. Woo was delighted, and left it to his underlings to look after the details.

The new sitting took place on 2 June 1994, in Snowdon's London studio. These pictures were being taken half a world away from Hong Kong. Would they look different? How much does location dictate tone or content? When we raised these questions with Snowdon's assistant, Graham Piggott, he explained that all the essential elements would be the same as those in Hong Kong. Before leaving for Hong Kong months before, Snowdon had decided upon camera and lens, and from the beginning had insisted the portraits be black and white. These photographs are about character and personality. Colour, however enriching, distracts from these subjects much the same way glasses detract from the face.

When we looked in Snowdon's small studio at the back of his London home, we found the same arrangement of lighting and camera as we had seen in Hong Kong. Graham said it would be impossible to calculate the number of times this equipment had circled the globe on one assignment or another. The backdrop is the most compelling element. Snowdon has used this same rust-coloured cloth for decades. In black and white the rich rust colour comes up a soft and resonant grey. It seems more fragile than it is and is soft to the touch – we suspect more from age than because of the material itself. And where did he find it? Is it an old theatre curtain or a painter's drop sheet? And how did it attain its rich and varied colour?

These are the tools, the framing devices, the separate elements that make up the stage upon which the subject sits. But it is to Snowdon that they must surrender, and achieving that capitulation is a large measure of his genius.

Woo arrived much more relaxed than he had been in Hong Kong, and the jockeying for control with Snowdon was good-humoured. Snowdon wanted to keep away from formality; no white shirts and ties. Woo wanted one shot in a blue shirt and tie; Snowdon deferred. Woo had forgotten his cuff links; Snowdon said not to worry, he could lend him a pair. They were gold, and bore Snowdon's family crest in red enamel. Woo put them on quickly, hardly noticing how beautiful they were, or how personal. Snowdon selected a tie from the half-dozen Woo had brought, and handed it to him. As he began to knot it, Snowdon smiled, and complimented him on how well he tied a Windsor knot. Woo looked blank. He was tying his tie the way he'd been taught. And cuff links are cuff links; nothing more, nothing less.

However, when he came out of the studio later, he was pleased. There would be pictures from the sitting that he would like. And, of course, there were; not because the photographs were better – Snowdon does not take any bad pictures – but because he had exercised more control over the time and place of the sitting, and had even won a compromise from Snowdon. His satisfaction came from greater control, not a more flattering portrait.

Corporate power is about control, about laying down commands which others hasten to carry out; at the very least, it is about imposing personal will over someone else. This is not a trait which can be put on or shuffled off; it emerges whether the tycoon is engineering a corporate takeover or butting heads with a renowned British photographer.

Three of the men in this chapter run three of the largest corporations in Hong Kong. Their backgrounds, personalities and ideas shape the corporate culture of the place. Cheng Yu-tung represents the old guard; he is still a hands-on operator of the huge development company he founded, New World Development Co. Ltd. Walter Kwok is Chairman and Chief Executive Officer of Sun Hung Kai Properties Ltd, a development company founded by his late father, Tak-sing Kwok. Peter Woo is Chairman of Wheelock, a huge conglomerate founded by his late father-in-law, Sir Y. K. Pao.

But the key to understanding the financial changes that have recently transformed Hong Kong lies in the person and accomplishments of Charles Lee, who was Chairman of the Stock Exchange from January 1992 until October 1994. He was replaced as Chairman by another son-in-law of Sir Y. K. (who had four daughters), Edgar Cheng. Small circles, interconnected by blood, marriage and the almighty dollar.

Peter Woo gives us the flavour of the place; Lee the insight into its mechanics. We will therefore begin our portraits with Lee, and come back to Peter Woo.

CHARLES LEE

Charles Lee played a critical role in the early 1970s in persuading the founders of corporations to take their companies public. The subsequent sale of shares generated the capital that made their astonishing growth through the 1970s and into the 1980s possible. This enabled Chinese-owned corporations to supersede the British hongs in size, and finally to dominate the corporate landscape of Hong Kong. Lee played the traditional role of comprador. He brought Western ideas to suspicious billionaires. He had the confidence of men who had started with nothing, and still spoke only Chinese. His influence changed the way they did business, and brought to the Hong Kong corporation power beyond the worlds of business and finance, and international stature.

How did he do this? He is a London-educated barrister, who drafted some of the basic rules and regulations governing the stock market, while working for the Hong Kong government in the late 1960s and early '70s. But it takes more than knowledge to convince men like Cheng Yu-tung, who operates from instinct and intuition. It takes trust.

Lee's accomplishment was to generate that trust, and to persuade local businessmen to launch themselves into what was for most of them an entirely new form of enterprise, the limited, public corporation. It is doubtful if Hong Kong would stand where she is today without this enterprise.

The difficulty with the hongs that were the instruments of the colony's early merchant princes was that they could not expand quickly enough to meet the new challenges of development. Moreover, their financial organization was that of the partnership, often with unlimited liability. If anything went wrong, the owners stood to lose everything they owned, a circumstance that dampens the ardour of even the most enthusiastic investor. The invention of the limited corporation in 1855 – William Gladstone himself shepherded the necessary legislation through the British House of Commons – solved part of the problem. The investor could lose only the money invested in shares; that was the limit of his liability.

However, the venture was still dependent for necessary loans on the kindness of bankers, a commodity in no greater abundance in Hong Kong than elsewhere. Bankers ask all those impertinent

A PUBLIC DUTY

I think the criticism of the old Stock Market Council was that it was run like a private club, but that is all gone. The Stock Exchange has a duty to safeguard the interest of the public, so we cannot simply safeguard the interest of members only, and look after the interests of the public at the same time.

Charles Lee

questions – and, even worse, pertinent ones. They want to know what the money is for, and what happened to the last batch, and other intrusive details. They also want money for their money, in the form of interest. Finally, and sometimes fatally, they can and do pull the plug on an enterprise as soon as they see, or hear, or guess that things are going awry.

How much better it would be to get money that was not so costly, and not so tied. The solution, as Western financiers discovered long since, is to issue shares in the company to the investing public, which brings in cash beyond the reach of bankers. The only drawback is that the investing public, like the banker, wants some information about what is happening inside the firm. There must be rules, and an oversight body – the Stock Exchange – to see that the rules are followed. If they are, investors will prosper, firms will grow, and those who wield corporate power can have the money they need in return for a minimal check on their operations. It is that wondrous modern commodity, Other People's Money. It was Lee who made these expansionary truths evident to the emerging entrepreneurial class in Hong Kong.

Charles Lee was born in Shanghai in 1936. His mother was from Guangzhou, and his father was born in Chiu Chow. His father completed his early schooling in Hong Kong before enrolling in the University of Shanghai. Lee's parents met and married in Shanghai and abandoned their studies. Lee's father had learned English at school in Hong Kong and soon found work in a Shanghai shipping company. Lee was enrolled in a Christian school, St Francis Xavier. He learned Cantonese from his parents, Shanghainese from his environment, and studied English and Mandarin at school. When he was thirteen, the family fled Shanghai for Hong Kong after it became clear that the Communists would win China's civil war:

> We left in May 1949. My father had an office in Hong Kong, so it was relatively easy for us to move. We had a foothold here. I was enrolled in another Christian school in Hong Kong run by Irish Jesuits. It was very tough.

Lee did not go on to university immediately. He decided instead to join an accounting firm:

> I qualified as an accountant at the age of twenty-three or twenty-four. The strange thing that happened to me was that the day I became a qualified accountant was the day I decided to leave the profession . . . I was thinking maybe I should do something else. I could not really see myself doing figures for the rest of my life. Anyway, I joined the government.

He stayed in government service for several years, and claims the experience taught him important lessons about organization and bureaucracy. As he explained, 'You learn very quickly how to get things done, or how not to get things done.'

After his stint in public service, Lee enrolled at London University and received a Master of Law degree from the London School of Economics and Political Science. His specialities were corporate law, company law, taxation, take-overs and mergers. Being a qualified accountant gave Lee a tremendous advantage in these fields, and when he returned to Hong Kong, he went back into government:

> Part of my job was to be the Secretary to the Company Law Revision Committee. We produced two reports. The first one on the protection of the investor which would result in the enactment of a securities order. The securities order was enacted in 1972, I think. The second report concerns company law. Most of the recommendations contained in that report have already been implemented. They were a series of amendments to company order.

When he left to enter into private law practice, he retained his position as Secretary to the Law Revision Committee on a voluntary basis, without pay. Lee wanted to finish off the work he had begun in office and was prepared to do it without remuneration.

GROW GENTLY, SWEET MARKET

For the market here, I would personally like to see that the market rises very gently. In the last few years we have seen sharp rises. Of course when you have a sharp rise a lot of people want to get out, and a lot of people want to get in. I am constantly asked the question, 'Is the market too high or is it time for me to sell?' But if it rises gently, I think it will be a healthy market for everyone.

Charles Lee

We were interviewing Charles Lee in Jardine House, the white edifice in Central with beautiful round windows. Whenever we enter a corporate office we scan desks, bookcases and walls for something personal, something we might use as a kind of key to the private self. There was a photo of a yacht on the wall. And the instant we remarked on how beautiful a boat it was, the serious mask and sober tone fell away to reveal an almost childlike rapture for a new toy. He went on to explain that he had recently bought a newer, bigger yacht, a 140-foot boat capable of crossing the Pacific, and substantial enough to land a helicopter on the front deck.

Lee explains that he became involved with the Stock Exchange and the securities market by accident, and that it was his accounting background and specialization in corporate law that made him valuable:

> *The securities market underwent a tremendous change in the 1970s. Before 1970, the market was a very quiet market, a very small market . . . There are two things one has to look at. First, there were very few listed companies in the early 1970s. Perhaps fifty or sixty companies. These were the big companies, the utilities like Hongkong Electric and China Light & Power – that sort of company. The local merchants had never even thought of going public. They certainly didn't know how to do it . . . I think it was really because of a lack of knowledge, and also a lack of confidence. They were not really sure that the market would accept them as a public company.*

But the atmosphere changed and these small local companies suddenly became very big. The real estate market took off, and the undeveloped land held by companies like New World Development, and Sun Hung Kai Properties, assured future investors that these firms would have assets to develop no matter how expensive land became:

> *It was in 1972 that they suddenly realized that going public was a very easy way to raise capital. And it is a cheap way to raise capital because it's not borrowed, and you don't have to repay it.*

The traditional way to raise capital was to go to the bank. But as we have seen, that put them under the scrutiny of the bank. And every fluctuation of property prices brought the banks down on their backs. They were never free to run their companies as they wished.

> *I represented most of these big local companies as a lawyer. I handled most of the flotations for them. A lot of them didn't even speak English. So, very often, I accompanied them to the bank when they had to borrow. The bank was usually quite happy to lend them money.*

87

They were all very solid companies. Often they had paid for the land outright, out of their own pockets. They were borrowing money for the building costs only, and offering the land as security.

Lee explained that the local companies moved very quickly into the market as soon as they realized the benefits of going public.

They saw me helping one family float their company and then asked me to help them float theirs . . . They were following the other's example. You see this a lot, you can find many examples of this sort of thing throughout the last twenty years. If one person does something, the other one follows . . . A lot of them would like to be the first. They don't like being the last. This is what happens in Hong Kong, if someone has a bright idea and it works, then immediately everybody copies it, and they move very fast.

Lee was often asked to sit on the boards of these new public companies. The families wanted to be sure they were following the rules and the best way to ensure that was to have the man who had set some of the rules sitting on their board. Lee admits that he felt under a lot of pressure from such potential conflict of interest, but says that he was never pressurized by one group to reveal the actions of another.

As Chairman of the Stock Exchange, Lee's task was to explain to these tycoons the duties and responsibilities of a director of a public company. They were no longer free to act exactly as they pleased. The company was receiving new capital to invest in ever-more-ambitious projects, money that didn't have to be paid back. But they were obliged to share much more than their profits with these new shareholders, they had to share information. It was a different kind of scrutiny, more palatable than that of the banks, but nonetheless it was still scrutiny.

In the beginning it was predominantly a domestic market, but it has undergone a dramatic change over the past few years, and the Hong Kong Stock Exchange now ranks sixth in the world in terms of the total value of the market: behind Paris, and ahead of Toronto. Lee points out that approximately fifty per cent of the liquidity is provided by international investors. Initially, there was concern that international investment would de-stabilize the market, that at the slightest hint of scandal or political turmoil it would pull out and the whole market would collapse. But the international investor's attitude towards Hong Kong has changed as much as Hong Kong has changed over the past twenty years. Fund managers now look at the Hong Kong market as a place for long-term investment, no longer simply a place to make a quick buck. The market is also now playing a major role in China's modernization:

You have on one hand international investors keen to invest in China, and on the other China's enterprises, which need huge amounts of capital to modernize their equipment . . . But the two don't meet. The investors are not comfortable to go directly into China; they don't know how the companies are being run, or whom they are dealing with . . . We went to China and suggested that we could help bring some of these companies up to international standards. The Chinese accepted our help, because they know they have to reach the international community. It is becoming a new role for us to play, to regulate those companies and ensure that they meet international standards . . .

The lessons Charles Lee taught Hong Kong have now to be learned by China.

CHENG YU-TUNG

The greatest fortunes usually come from ideas. Henry Ford's was an idea about mass production, Sam Walton's about volume retail sales and Bill Gates' about easy access to computer technology. However, Hong Kong's great fortunes come from opportunity, not ideas. The prescient founders of the great development companies understood that shortage of land, and an ever-increasing population, were a recipe for gold. Li Ka-shing may have started in plastics, and Sir Y. K. Pao in shipping, but all have eventually moved into property development to clear the last hurdle from ordinary wealth to billionaire status.

If the family fortune is on the scale of a Ford or a Walton, it's not likely to go from rags to riches to rags in three generations. It may diminish over time, but the founder's idea often replenishes the till well into the third generation. But what of the opportunist's hoard? The founder has the instincts to turn a set of circumstances into huge wealth, but when he passes, he takes those instincts to the grave. The family is left a fortune, but not the tools to keep it growing. The Hunt family of Texas is the best example of this. The children inherited a financial empire and hubris, and now they are just ordinary millionaires.

What will happen when the children of Hong Kong's billionaires take the wheel? Most of the founders are still in control, and approaching seventy. They surrender only to death, not to boardroom politics or ambitious sons. Cheng Yu-tung is one of the old guard. His fortune and story are pure rags to riches Hong Kong. He briefly ceded control to his son Henry Cheng. He was going to retire and play golf. Mistakes were made. Momentum was lost. He returned.

We interviewed him in his offices at the New World Tower, 18 Queen's Road Central. The offices had been recently refurbished. They had a very familiar feel about them; the same decorator had worked on the interior of one of his prize holdings, the Grand Hyatt Hong Kong, at 1 Harbour Road.

The interview was conducted in Cantonese, without translation. One of us (Evelyn Huang) interviewed; the other (Lawrence Jeffery) listened, and watched. Stewart Leung, Group General Manager of New World Development, led us into the office and sat with us during the interview. Cheng Yu-tung did not enter with a secretary at his side; he

DEMOCRACY = INEFFICIENCY

When the Chinese economy opens up, everything will be good. The more democracy we have, the worse the economy will be. If you want to have greater economic efficiency, you will have to have less democracy.

Cheng Yu-tung

did not run his own tape recorder, or have notes taken.

His voice preceded him. It is loud and forceful, like Li Ka-shing's, but with a more limited range. Cheng is similar in age and build to Li Ka-shing. But there is a fundamental difference; where Li Ka-shing is precision, control and intellect, Cheng Yu-tung is all instinct, animal magnetism and force. There is a palpable physical strength and presence to the man.

The most puzzling moment occurred when he greeted Evelyn Huang. In a millisecond his eyes scanned her fingers, wrist, neck and lapel. Later, we realized that this was a jeweller's eye, a remnant of his early years working for his father-in-law at Chow Tai Fook Jewellery Co. He assessed in the blink of an eye. When an art dealer enters a room, he or she scans the walls for interesting paintings, the photographer looks at a scene and wonders about the light, but the jeweller masters the quickest take.

Cheng Yu-tung was born in Shunde, in Guangdong Province in 1925. His family was very poor, and he started work at the age of fourteen:

> *I went to Macao. I could not get accustomed to it. In a way it was like leaving my homeland . . . Today you can travel by car and cover the distance in two hours. Back in those days, it took a minimum of two days. I first took a boat, and then rode on the back seat of a bicycle, criss-crossing paths amidst paddy fields. There were plenty of bandits, and of course I was afraid . . . At that time you had to be brave. We were almost without food.*

His first job was as an apprentice in a goldsmith shop. He helped with the general cleaning, swept the floor, prepared tea, and helped open the shop for business every morning. He stayed in Macao until the end of World War II, when he moved to Hong Kong.

Just before that, Cheng had returned to his native village in China to marry the daughter of his uncle, his first cousin. Her father was one of three owners of Chow Tai Fook Jewellery, and Cheng was sent to oversee a branch of the firm in Hong Kong.

> *Chow Tai Fook was started in Guangzhou. When the Japanese invaded China [1937], it was moved to Macao. Two or three years after that another Chow Tai Fook shop was opened in Hong Kong. The business continued in Hong Kong during the Japanese occupation, with the help of two or three shop assistants. At the end of the war, my uncle sent me to Hong Kong to look after the business.*

Cheng never intended to go out and start his own business. He worked hard and Chow Tai Fook grew. His father-in-law wanted to retire, but his sons were still too young to take over. The other partners also wanted to pull out, so the founders decided to sell to Cheng:

92

DO NOT CONFRONT CHINA

China has already said very clearly that it will not interfere. The question is do you believe in this? Yes. So long as we do not confront China or cause China to lose face. Even today China will do its best to help Hong Kong. Do not confront China, for if you do, China will not be happy at heart.

Cheng Yu-tung

SOLIDARITY

I do not know enough about the situation in North America. However, there is a group of people in Hong Kong who are in constant contact with each other in person or through the telephone to discuss important issues and agree to jointly take action. I am not saying that people in North America do not have a sense of solidarity. I dare not say so. But there are people in Hong Kong who are willing to try to help.

Cheng Yu-tung

93

I bought the business in 1955 or 1956. I cannot remember easily, business was already very good. It was in 1957 that I started a small real estate business with friends. It was really a very small-scale operation. We would buy one or two old buildings and have them demolished and redeveloped and sell at a profit. We would re-invest these profits in other development projects. It was a very small undertaking.

By the 1960s, his firms were flourishing. The riots in Hong Kong in 1967 brought a downturn in the property market and ruined many companies but Cheng never believed the troubles would last, or that China wanted to see Hong Kong hurt:

The riots were not caused by China, just disturbances instigated under the guise of the Communists. You see, there were no military installations in Hong Kong. If China wanted to take back Hong Kong, it could do so without having to cause a disturbance. Hong Kong would not know what to do if the Chinese government were to cut off the supply of water or food.

One of Cheng's highest-profile developments, and one that completely revolutionized the look of the Kowloon waterfront, began in the late 1970s:

TAXES

Unlikely to have a lot of investments overseas. I do not have a lot of interest in this because returns on investment are not good. First, taxes are much higher. Why should I do it? Right.

Cheng Yu-tung

A wharf stood on the present site, and a railway track ran through it. I had checked with the government and knew that there was no longer a need for a railway there. I knew it had to be developed. So I bought the wharf. Soon the government decided the area should be developed. I had discussions with them. The government said that this was a prime site in Tsim Sha Tsui and that they wanted an impressive world-class project there. They asked me if I was willing to employ a world-class architect to draw up the plans and not just a Hong Kong architect. I agreed. I asked the government to grant me some more land and I would come up with a really world-class project.

The site now holds the New World Centre, the New World Hotel and a shopping centre. Cheng constructed a concrete walk along the edge of the Kowloon waterfront that starts at the New World Hotel and ends at the Star Ferry docks. It is one of the most beautiful pedestrian walks in the world. It is often crowded with teenagers and young couples late into the night. It is a place where they might find a little space, a beautiful view. The view of Hong Kong at night, with the lights of the buildings and neon signs bouncing from Victoria Harbour to the low flying clouds and back again, is stunning.

Cheng claims that he presently has three per cent of his company's assets invested in China but that he intends to increase that to a maximum of twenty per cent.

Why do I invest in China? My serious investment in China started after the 4 June incident [Tiananmen Square] . . . The present-day deputy mayor of Guangzhou is a very good friend of mine. I have known him for over ten years. He was formerly the Party secretary in my

DEMOCRACY AND WELFARE

If we talk of democracy, then we talk of welfare, etc. Of course if I were to stand for election as a councillor, then I can campaign in housing estates with promises. I can promise people assistance in case they are unemployed, I can promise to give old age pensions when one reaches a certain age, etc. But what happens then? Where does the money come from? From our businessmen. Do we not have to impose heavy taxes? Taxes are now very high in Canada. Canada still has a deficit. It is because there are too many of those people. You support those people who do not go to work. But people in Hong Kong are all hard-working. They are all very hard-working. That is why we are so successful today.

Cheng Yu-tung

LEARNING

Even when I was very young, I had always wanted to learn from others. In the past, people thought that I was lazy, but in fact this was not the case. If I manage a company, I would go to visit those shops doing good business. We were in the same business and we knew each other, so I would chat with them. I wanted to find out why their business was so good. First, it could very well be that the shops were in good locations, or that the chief shop assistants were offering excellent service. It could be that the merchandise offered was of good quality, and that even the very best goods could be made available. I learnt from them. Similarly, I would also go to visit shops with poor business to find out why business was bad.

Cheng Yu-tung

native village. Before 4 June the Chinese government had built a power generating plant and was in the process of building a highway in Guangzhou . . . It was about one-third completed. The Chinese government introduced austerity after 4 June. But you cannot tighten up on road building. So the deputy mayor came to discuss this with me. He asked if I were interested we would work together. I said fine, for my view was that roads and transportation would always be required.

Cheng ended the interview stressing the importance of charitable work. He argued that it was important to give back to the community what you get out of it. The areas he focuses on are education and medicine, especially in China. He is not happy when politics interrupt this good will:

The University of California informed me of a plan to send doctors from China to the United States to undertake research work for two years. I gave the money for their return air tickets and salary so that they could do research work at the University of California . . . Unfortunately, after the 4 June incident, many of these people did not want to return home. I was very disappointed. Recently, the Chancellor of the University came to discuss this issue with me and I told him that if they did not go back, I would withdraw my support for this project . . . It is not good that they do not want to return. My aim is that they should return to China to contribute to her medical advancement . . .

Cheng Yu-tung arrived at the Royal Garden Hotel in a cream-coloured Rolls-Royce bearing the lucky licence-plate number 8888. He was accompanied by a tall, strikingly attractive young woman, who carried the golf shirts he intended to wear in a shopping bag. This was the only subject who did not speak English. Somehow, Snowdon persuaded Cheng to abandon his golf shirts, and wear an Issey Miyake shirt. And somehow, alone in the studio together, they spoke.

95

WALTER KWOK

Walter Kwok was born in Hong Kong in 1950. He is the Chairman and Chief Executive Officer of Sun Hung Kai Properties. His brother Thomas, born in 1951, is Vice-Chairman and Managing Director; brother Raymond, born in 1952, is also Vice-Chairman and Managing Director. The brothers took control of Sun Hung Kai Properties upon the death of their father, Tak-sing Kwok, in 1990.

We spent the day of 1 January 1993 on Walter's new Italian yacht, with his wife Wendy, their three young children, and his mother-in-law, Pola Lee. As we pulled out of the Causeway Bay typhoon shelter, Walter pointed out the twin spires of the recently completed Central Plaza building. It is the tallest building in Asia, and the fourth tallest building in the world.

Walter pointed it out because they built it, not because they own it. Ownership is irrelevant. Walter is pure entrepreneur. Business is forward movement; it is dealing, connecting and assembling the pieces of ever-more-complex puzzles, and juggling ever-more-intricately interconnected elements.

To most of us, assets are something we might live off of in old age, or cash-in in desperate times. We protect them in vaults, and pay solemn experts to tell us of their health and viability. For Walter Kwok, the acquisition of assets is meaningless if they are not immediately put into play. For the Kwok brothers, and entrepreneurs of their generation and energy, assets are only a fuel feeding Hong Kong's insatiable economic engines. And this generation's drug of choice? Adrenalin.

Tak-sing Kwok started with an import/export business in Guangzhou. He moved his business to Macao after the Japanese occupation of China, and settled in Hong Kong after the end of World War II. His son Walter returned to Hong Kong from university in 1972. He had a degree in Civil Engineering and came back to Hong Kong to complete the practical training necessary to qualify as a professional engineer. His father wanted him to work outside of the family business for a few years, so Kwok went to work for Gordon Lee, a long-time associate of his father, and a man he says inspired him to become an engineer.

Kwok is a big, shy, easy-going man. It is impossible to look at his face and have any idea of what he thinks. His wife explains by saying that he is very Chinese, he is not Westernized like others of his generation, even though he spent years studying in the West. Where Tim Fok and Peter Woo are open and gregarious, Kwok is withdrawn. He is more comfortable with other

Chinese than with Westerners. Peter Woo's handshake is aggressive, almost painful, Tim Fok's is perfunctory but polite, but Walter Kwok's is so indifferent as to be almost non-existent. Kwok meets and greets with his eyes. They are powerful and penetrating. They can be warm and friendly, coolly indifferent, or they can brighten with an intellectual or emotional force that is startling. This is a powerful face and a face one would not want to see angry.

When he finally joined his father's firm, his first tasks were to supervise construction sites, work with architects and handle general project management. But this was not so much

FAMILY SIZE

I think we are lucky in that we are a small family. I mean compared to others, other families in Hong Kong. Our family size is fairly small, three boys and one girl, and so basically we are very close. My father had been able to talk to us, and we were able to spend time with him.

Walter Kwok

apprenticeship as his introduction to an ever-increasing responsibility. The apprenticeship had been carefully supervised by his father years before. Every Sunday the family would gather together at a Chiu Chow restaurant for lunch. When lunch was finished, Tak-sing Kwok would drive his wife and sons to a newly purchased piece of property, or a building site under construction. He would take the boys through all of the stages of development, point out problems and innovations. To this day, before making a major purchase in the colony, the three Kwok brothers bring their mother to the site for her opinion and consent. The family claims that the senior Mrs Kwok has an encyclopedic memory, and can remember the prices of every site and the cost of development.

Kwok started into the family business at a dramatic time. In 1972 the stock market index went up to a record high of 1,700, but collapsed to 100 by year's end:

> *It was a very bad time. A lot of people got wiped out. There had been too much speculation . . . And of course the collapse of the stock market affected everything else.*

The crash signalled the end of the beginning of the development boom. Hong Kong had been very much a manufacturing-based economy throughout the 1950s and 1960s. The 1970s saw the beginnings of the financial industry, the growth of a renewed stock market and the dominance of property development.

> *We were not involved in the stock market, we were not speculators. My father still had his import/export business, and even though there were problems in Hong Kong, the world-wide economy was good.*

Tak-sing Kwok was the agent for Y. K. K. Zippers, which account for seventeen per cent of the world's zipper market:

> *My father's manufacturing business did not suffer. But when the stock market collapsed, the land prices came down. Because confidence was shaken. Not shaken, shattered. He felt that in the long term, the economy would be good. He felt that this collapse was only a temporary thing. It was about speculation. Like somebody caught a cold . . . So he bought up a lot of land at that time.*

Kwok says that his father was always very independent-minded. He would listen to the news, and read extensively, but would not always follow the expert's advice. He had his own way of analysing information, and when he reached a conclusion and came to a decision, he stuck to it. But Kwok credits hard work more than instinct, and says that his father worked seven days a week, and that work was his hobby, his life, everything:

> *I only work six days a week. And I take holidays. My father never took a holiday. He never went away except on business. The only time he took off was for Chinese New Years. But*

99

everybody takes that day off – it's like Christmas . . . I have some hobbies. I like scuba-diving and hiking, and boating. I like to swim. He didn't have anything like that.

We were interrupted by a phone call. He spent more time listening than talking. During the five-minute call he spoke only three or four sentences. It had been one of his brothers. He also has a sister, who is not involved in the business:

When my father began his property development business in the 1960s, he would take us to visit sites, see the countryside, see the properties, and see other people's properties. On Sundays, he would get the three boys and drive us around the whole day.

The most important thing he learned from his father was how much joy he got from work. And when times were bad he never despaired; he simply worked harder. The Kwoks have only been serious investors in China since 1992:

We all thought after Tiananmen Square that the Conservatives had won, and that China would probably go backwards rather than forward. That was not true. The Conservatives won, but the open door policy continues. It has become even more favourable to outside investors.

The younger generation viewed Tiananmen as a setback, but the older generation of businessmen, men like Cheng Yu-tung, felt the underlying economic force behind China's forward movement would not be so easily stopped. The Kwoks realized that they really had no choice but to invest in the mainland. They have worked hard to learn how to deal with partners there, and government officials, and are all now studying Mandarin. We asked him about the difference between doing business in Hong Kong and doing business in China:

In Hong Kong, it is very much the Western way. In Hong Kong, if you want to do a joint venture, it is very complicated, and detailed, and you have to publish it. But in China if you have a joint venture you can write out the specifics on three pages . . . It's the Chinese way. They have a lot of trust. They have principles. They don't go into the exact details of what you are doing, like the completion date . . . The problem is that you end up spending more time getting this done. What we can achieve in Hong Kong in one hour might take a day or two to complete in China.

Obviously, bureaucratic shuffling uses up whatever slack is created by the lack of details required on the mainland, and the job takes longer, in the end.

Kwok claims to have ten per cent of his companies' assets invested in China. When we asked him about the political dangers, he told us that people in China are more concerned about the economy than politics:

Government officials at the district or city level are now only concerned with economic goals. In the old days, they would talk about Communist ideology.

His children are still very young, and the question of succession is far, far away. When we ask him what he wants for his children, he speaks of the love his father had for his work. He wants us to understand this special joy and struggles to find the perfect comparison. Finally, he says he saw the same concentration, and love of the job at hand, in Snowdon's eyes. It was something he noticed, something he was struck by and remembers:

I would like them to continue in the family business. But it is up to them . . . If someone doesn't like to do it no matter how hard you try to persuade them, they won't do it . . . I hope they will but if they don't I will understand. But my understanding of my children is that

they will . . . You have to like it. You have to be aggressive. You have to have the desire to be number one, to be first in whatever you do. You have to be a perfectionist . . . If they don't have that in their eyes, then I don't think they can do it . . .

We joined the Kwok family one last time for Sunday lunch at a favourite Chiu Chow restaurant. The senior Mrs Kwok spends each Sunday with a different son. This Sunday she was with Walter and Wendy and her grandchildren. There are also a few close business associates at the table. Everyone is dressed casually. It is hard to imagine that Walter and these executives run such a huge conglomerate. There is none of the tension, the posing and positioning we have come to expect in a gathering of such executives. We are told this is very Chinese.

The food arrives. Chiu Chow food is from Swatow, and reflects the history of the region. It is a history of suffering and privation. Nothing has been wasted. We are served boiled blood, deep-fried intestines, and sautéed bone marrow. This is a diet designed to take advantage of every morsel, the diet of the poor. And it is food of choice for one of the richest families in the world.

PETER WOO

There could be no greater contrast of personalities than between those of Walter Kwok and Peter Woo. The Kwok succession suggests that there has been no real succession but a transfer from one generation to the next. The style and spirit of management, and the degree of the family's involvement in every aspect of the business, have not changed since the passing of the founder. And there is no reason to suspect that there will be any real change until this generation hands the business to the next.

Peter Woo is a fascinating, highly intelligent and extremely complex figure on the corporate landscape. His confidence and bearing seem American, not Chinese. He has the intellectual power of Li Ka-shing, but is not as wary, cautious or subtle about how he uses it. Woo uses his intellect aggressively, like a young man showing off his muscles; display means more than delivery. It is clear he does not suffer fools at all.

The interview was held in the penthouse of Wheelock House. He does not have a secretary taking notes or his own tape recorder. Benny Chan, a trusted advisor, sits opposite. Chan explains that Woo is pressed for time and will probably have to leave early. This has been used on us before. If the interview goes badly or becomes awkward, an excuse for ending it is always close at hand, but it didn't happen this time.

Woo was the favourite son-in-law of the late Sir Y. K. Pao. When Sir Y. K. died in 1991, Woo took the helm. And now, not yet fifty, he has stepped aside as Chairman of the holding company, Wheelock. He holds the title of Honorary Chairman but he is too young and too ambitious to have reached all of his goals. What might he be setting his sights on now?

He was born in Shanghai in 1946. In 1949, the family moved to Hong Kong, where he attended St Stephen's Primary School and College from 1954 to 1964. He graduated from the University of Cincinnati in Ohio, with majors in Physics and Mathematics, and went on to complete an MBA at Columbia Business School. After Columbia, he went into commercial banking at the Chase Manhattan Bank, then he joined Sir Y. K. Pao's Worldwide Shipping Group as Executive Director in 1975. He met and married Betty, one of Sir Y. K. Pao's four daughters. Woo's father was an architect and wanted his son to join the family firm. Woo studied architecture for three years before changing

EMOTION

I think actions are prompted by emotions, but when you actually do it, you have to execute it intelligently.
Peter Woo

direction. He says he didn't like the idea that his destiny was not in his own hands. The client always had the final word:

> *I called my father long distance. I said, 'Well, Dad, I tried, I like it, but I really have to tell you that I don't want to be an architect' . . . He took it very well. It took a lot of courage to make that call. The response was very cordial. It was a big relief.*

He says he wanted to become a banker from an early age, because he felt banking was the best training for business. But bankers are discreet, and though they have tremendous influence, they tend to keep a very low profile. Unlike many of his contemporaries who left Hong Kong to go to school in the United States or the United Kingdom, Woo was politically active and involved, and was elected Senior Class President in his graduating year.

He claims that the trader mentality dominates Hong Kong. People are clannish and remain in a closed circle of friends and associates. It is not that they are unfriendly – they would entertain a foreigner if they had to – but they don't make a point of going outside of this small circle. It was Sir Y. K. Pao who convinced him to be a more international and outward-looking person:

> *I was working at a bank when I married. A few years later Sir Y. K. Pao came to me and said, 'My fleet is getting bigger and I would like you to come and help out.' That's really how I started. He was a tremendous influence on me from a business standpoint, and from a personal standpoint as a mentor.*

AN INTERNATIONAL GAME

**Sir Y. K. Pao was the
only Hong Kong business person
to be successful competing in the
international arena. Shipping is an
international game. Most Hong Kong
people who invested overseas lost
their money, except him. He had
made a lot of money, and brought
the money back to invest
in Hong Kong.**

Peter Woo

Pao was also from Shanghai, and had started in the shipping business in 1956. When he began he could barely speak a word of English. By the time of his death, he was the most international and sophisticated of the old guard and played golf with prime ministers and presidents around the world. He had built up a shipping fleet with a capacity of twenty-one million tons by 1974. Even at its peak, the fleet of the Greek shipping magnate Aristotle Onassis had less than four million tons.

Peter Woo gained a reputation for being something of a tyrant in his early days with Pao.

I think that you have to realize that my position before was Managing Director. Now I'm Chairman. I think that the person evolved, a person grew; basically, a person develops with the job.

Woo speaks with tremendous affection and admiration for Sir Y. K. Pao. When business declined, Pao was able to reduce his tonnage from twenty-one million tons to ten million tons without losing his nerve or surrendering control of the business. He followed his instincts, and when the market hit the bottom in 1981, Pao was the first to order six new tankers at US $35 million each. Their value soon doubled. He was the first one out of the bad market, and the first one in when the market recovered. Woo says:

When I first went into shipping I enrolled in a special business course. We were asked what was the most important objective of a shipping company. All these businessmen said, 'Well you have to maximize shareholder's value.' Wrong! . . . Survival! It's all about survival.

While Woo, in his new position as Honorary Chairman of the firm gives due weight to the notion that his shareholders receive maximum value for their investment, throughout our conversation he has stressed the importance of development and growth. He is most moved by Sir Y. K. Pao's steely determination, nerve, and eventual triumph against the odds. And when he speaks of his children, he says he hopes they have a complete education and are able to develop to their greatest potential.

This is all about confrontation – with others and oneself. And it is about personal growth and the reach for ever-greater challenges. But survival is the real challenge, and question, for a man whose life seems to have been preparation for a future as yet unknown . . . This is someone to watch.

A CHEERLEADER

**I believe college is a growing
up place where you mature, where
you make friends, and where you
really develop your personal
characteristics, and personal skills.
That's why I became very active in
school. I was a cheerleader.**

Peter Woo

WOMEN OF POWER:

WESTERN SEXISM, EASTERN CULTURE

SOME PEOPLE SEEM TO KNOW WHAT WILL HAPPEN TO ME. ONE OF THEM IS ONE OF OUR FORMER GOVERNORS, LORD MACLEHOSE . . . HE WAS IN HONG KONG ON HIS WAY TO CHINA IN MARCH LAST YEAR. HE CAME TO THE LEGISLATIVE COUNCIL TO DISCUSS THE POLITICAL SITUATION WITH US. AND, OF COURSE, WE ALL AGREED TO DISAGREE. I MEAN, MACLEHOSE'S VIEWS AND MINE ARE LIKE CHALK AND CHEESE. THERE WAS A DINNER PARTY. AFTER DINNER HE CAME OVER AND SAID, 'EMILY, LET'S SIT DOWN AND HAVE A COFFEE.' HE SAT DOWN AND STARTED TALKING ABOUT VISITING A PRISON IN CHINA A FEW YEARS EARLIER. HE SAID THE CONDITIONS WERE VERY BAD. AND HE SAID THAT THE PAPERS OF THE PRISONERS WERE ALL IN DISARRAY, MEANING THAT ONCE YOU'RE THROWN IN, NOBODY HEARS FROM YOU AGAIN. HE SAID THAT THE ONLY THING THE PRISONERS HAD TO LOOK FORWARD TO WAS IF THEY HAD A VISITOR, AND IF THE PRISONER WAS REALLY VERY LUCKY, THE VISITOR MIGHT GIVE HIM SOME CIGARETTES. AND THEN HE TURNED AND LOOKED AT ME AND HE SAID, 'EMILY, IN THE FUTURE WHEN YOU ARE IN PRISON I WILL COME AND VISIT YOU. I WILL BRING YOU SOME CIGARETTES.' HE WAS NOT SMILING . . . I WAS QUITE STUNNED, AND I WAS QUITE ANGRY.

Emily Lau

It is not lack of recognition that disturbs me but my own limitations.

Emily Lau is the angriest woman in Hong Kong. She is angry about a lot of things, perhaps too angry to be effective. But her anger and resentment at the condescending attitude of a former Governor may be justified, and typical of the anger that is partly responsible for making the women in this chapter so remarkable.

Privately, the influence and authority of women within the family is undeniable; publicly, it is something else again. Anson Chan and Baroness Dunn have achieved success within the system, but the women in this chapter have succeeded by defying the system, and society's expectations, and define themselves through their own particular achievements. Each of these women has taken the energy of anger and channelled it into a potent force. This is not to diminish Emily Lau's achievement, or to suggest that she does not have an important role to play in the future. She is an elected member of the Legislative Council, and one of the most fearless, articulate and energetic individuals on the political landscape. She lacks the backing and support of a broadly based and carefully organized political party, but she was elected by an impressive majority of her constituents. Clearly, she touches a nerve. For women, it is a nerve worn raw by a patriarchal society still uncomfortable with a woman who voices her opinion publicly; and for men it is the lingering resentment of British colonial attitude typified by Lord MacLehose's imperious attitude. Imperialism, and colonialism, can only be rationalized if the dominating power sees all others as intellectually and morally inferior. In fact, it can be argued that the women of Hong Kong have good reason to be twice as angry as the men.

But these women, and the women of Hong Kong, are too complicated to be defined by anger alone. We are not sociologists or anthropologists and have neither the inclination nor the expertise to discuss the women of Hong Kong in such contexts. We can, however, stitch together a portrait of the women of Hong Kong by exploring differences in attitude between generations, and noticing similarities or differences to women in the West. Obviously, most of the women we have interviewed are highly intelligent and sophisticated. They are world travellers. And their education, language and comportment are more British than anything else.

The first thing we noticed was how firmly held and maintained are family ties and friendships. This has a great deal to do with Confucianism and *guanxi*. Where men use *guanxi*, or connections, primarily for business, women use it to maintain personal, intimate and emotional relationships. But it was still striking to see how connections left almost dormant for decades could be ignited by a single overseas call. Baroness Dunn, Anson Chan and Evelyn Huang were at school together. When these three women came together after decades of separation, and the many trials of marriage, children and careers, it was as if no time at all had passed. This is reflex behaviour, not learned, and they seem unaware of how rare it is for such relationships to last unaltered over such a long period of time.

But what of cross-generational conflicts, or transformations? One of the most moving stories we heard was relayed to us by Dr Li Shu-pui, the 92-year-old Superintendent of the Hong Kong Sanatorium and Hospital in Happy Valley. We had been discussing medical insurance, which is neither popular nor common in Hong Kong. To insure against illness seems to tempt fate. Of course there are other reasons why health insurance is unpopular there: a lingering reliance on more traditional Chinese health practices not covered by such insurance, a basic stubborn resistance to change, and pride – if you can't afford to get sick, don't get sick. We asked Dr Li what would happen if a patient could no longer afford treatment. He told us that the government covered those people who were without means, or whose money had run out. He then told us the story of a woman who had been terminally ill for a long period of time. She and her husband were in their early seventies, their children were grown up and gone, and her husband still ran his small business. They were moderately wealthy. As her illness progressed her medical bills began to eat into their savings. Eventually, her husband was forced to sell his business. Finally, he mortgaged their flat. At this rate, all their assets would be gone before her illness had run its course. A friend suggested the husband divorce his wife. If he divorced his wife she would be without means and therefore qualify for government assistance. This would save the last of their assets. The husband decided that this was the most reasonable option, and would allow them to keep their home. He initiated divorce proceedings. When the wife found out what he had done she pulled the intravenous drip from her arm, and the oxygen mask from her mouth. She lapsed into a coma and died.

Dr Li explained that she was a very traditional Chinese woman and had killed herself out of shame over the divorce, not because she was indigent. To lose money – for one reason or another – is bad luck, but to lose a husband to divorce is shameful. It's not likely that younger generations of Hong Kong women should feel such shame over divorce or separation. When we interviewed a group of university students we found both men and women coolly practical about marriage. The young women spoke of marriage as an event only slightly more significant in meaning than graduation, or the purchase of a first home. Have traditional values been eroded by the high pressure practicalities of modern life, or has the agenda changed?

Dr Li told us that one of the most satisfying aspects of his long medical career came from family counselling. He could probably provide an anecdote to illustrate perfectly every shift or change in the history of the women in Hong Kong. There remains one constant, however, and that is the case of the distressed wife of the middle-aged man in crisis. Dr Li said that many men find themselves taking up with a 'sing-song' girl when they reach middle age. The distressed wife would come to Dr Li for advice on what to do. He says that the best advice he could offer was for them to be patient and wait it out. If she divorces him she'll only lose – he'll get half the money and the 'sing-song' girl – and she'll end up bearing the shame of divorce. Wait him out, and then make a decision to stay or leave him. The 'sing-song' girl will get tired of him and find a richer, younger man. He says the men almost always return depressed and ashamed.

Dr Li's advice seems practical but hardly fair. Do the women of Hong Kong feel as strongly about marriage, and the shame of divorce, as the women in his stories? It is hard to tell. But when Baroness Dunn announced she was leaving Hong Kong for London she explained she was simply being a traditional wife and following her husband, the former Attorney General of Hong Kong, Michael Thomas, to his retirement in London. Obviously, there were other reasons, but this is the one to which she admitted.

What of the women in this chapter, then, and their struggle between head and heart? They are all energized by the anger that grows from injustice – towards themselves, their sex, or society at large. Has this anger shaped their hearts as much as their heads? It would be presumptious to try and compare their personal lives to their high-profile public lives. They have been enormously successful in those public lives – achievements that have put them in this book. Their private lives are a different matter, varied, complex, and not so clearly successful.

One has been happily married for almost sixty years. Two have been divorced. One has never married, and one seems to be doing just fine balancing husband, children and high-profile career. Divorce is usually seen as some sort of failure. But could it not be seen in a more positive light, as a rational accommodation of changing personal needs?

These issues are far too complicated to explore in detail here, but are often overlooked when searching for the reasons behind the success of extraordinary individuals. And are their private lives the result of the price they had to pay to achieve what they did? Would we be asking this question if these subjects were men? Not likely. Men seem to accept that there is a price to pay for almost everything. It becomes a question of how much, not why. We do know that children, family, husbands and friends dominate the thoughts of these women. They are seen as equal to career and success – not rival.

ELLEN LI

She wore a traditional *cheung sam* for her sitting with Lord Snowdon. She has been married to Dr Li Shu-pui since 1936, and has raised three children. She plays mahjong for money four or five times a week and rationalizes her losses by saying she loses less than most spend on cigarettes. She is a very traditional Chinese woman, and yet the woman who has done more to change the structure of the Chinese family in Hong Kong than perhaps any other single individual.

She has fought long and hard to change marriage and family laws, and in 1971 saw a new law passed abolishing the legal status of concubines. Under the laws of the Qing dynasty (1634–1911) a man could take a second wife or concubine if he had good reason. The most accepted argument was that his first wife had not produced a son or heir. Li's own father had three sons by a concubine. She is not bitter; she treated them as brothers, helped raise them, and supported them through medical school.

It is not surprising that she would have encouraged her three half-brothers to enter medicine. Her husband's brother, Dr Li Shu-fan, was one of the founders of the Hong Kong Sanatorium and Hospital in the early 1920s, the only privately owned hospital in Hong Kong. It has 500 beds, and overlooks the Happy Valley racecourse. It is the Li family business. Dr Li, born in 1903, still works five days a week as Superintendent of the hospital, and Ellen holds a seat on the Board of Directors.

Before we sat down to interview Ellen Li, the Lis took us on an extensive tour of the hospital. They took the greatest pleasure in showing us the luxury suite they had recently completed on an upper floor. It is the size of a large suite in a five-star hotel. There are two bedrooms, one with a standard hospital bed for the patient, the adjacent room for wife, husband or 'friend'. The most striking feature is a large picture window with an extraordinary view of Happy Valley racecourse. A pair of binoculars sits at the ready on an occasional table. We asked if this was not perhaps too stressful a distraction for the patient, and were told that if a patient has a bad heart, 'we close the blinds'.

The Lis have remained a remarkably close couple in spite of the demands their busy careers have made on their time and energy. We asked Dr Li a number of times how he felt about his wife. He was

MODIFIED PASSION

It was definitely not really love at first sight. But I just looked at him and I thought he was kind of all right, I guess. I liked his personality . . . And we see eye to eye on most things.

Ellen Li

non-committal. We pressed him; we knew what Ellen Li meant to Hong Kong; we wanted to know what she meant to him. He finally answered that he would be nothing without her. He would feel cut in half by her loss – a one-legged man standing in the middle of a room, unable to move, nowhere to go, and nothing to lean on.

Ellen Li was born in Saigon in 1908. Her parents were from Fukien Province, China, but met and married in Saigon while her father was the chief cashier at a rice mill there. He prospered and soon owned his own mill. Her brother, Yin Sheung, was eleven years old when she was born. She says that her father was delighted to have a daughter, and always treated her fairly:

At home it didn't make any difference if I was a boy or a girl. My father treated me like a boy so I learned how to bicycle, how to ride a horse, do all the things the boys did.

Li's father had unbound her mother's feet when they were married. Small feet were a sign of refinement and wealth. Only the rich could afford to have their women so crippled that they were unable to do even the most basic chores. It was also claimed that bound feet left lotus-like prints on the ground. It is certain no wife would wander far from home on such painful deformities:

When I was twelve or thirteen, my mother tried to get me to wear these cotton socks with no elasticity in them. You put them on and your feet can't expand. She thought that was a way to keep my feet small. But I didn't want to do it so I took them off. She didn't try to bind my feet, she tried to confine them a little bit. It is not good for a girl to have big feet.

Her father enrolled her in a boy's school in Saigon. It wasn't until she entered St Stephen's Girls' College in Hong Kong in 1924 that she finally came into contact with other girls:

When I first went to St Stephen's, I found that girls were quite different from boys. Girls were narrow-minded and jealous. I had never experienced that or felt that before. If you said something they didn't like, a woman would give you a long face; a man would fight with you.

Li spent three years at St Stephen's before enrolling in the University of Shanghai. She took business courses because her father wanted her to complete a degree in Business Administration. He hoped she would join her elder brother in the family business.

It was during her time at Shanghai University that her father's business failed. There was a seaman's strike in Hong Kong. Rice from Vietnam was exported to Hong Kong for sale or re-export to China. In the hot, humid climate, rice could not be stored for very long before it

112

INDEPENDENCE

I think education is the most important thing. And you must try to get financial independence. In my mother's time women couldn't divorce because they had no means; they were financially dependent. It was one of my father's beliefs, to give his daughter financial independence. So if your husband doesn't treat you well and you want a divorce you can go. You can live.

Ellen Li

began to rot. She says her father lost several million dollars and after the business went bankrupt he decided to sell all his holdings and retire to China.

Li completed her studies and applied for a job at an American bank in Shanghai. However, the Japanese attacked Shanghai in January 1932 to force the government to break an unofficial boycott of Japanese goods, and she left the city to return to her parents' village of Shek Ma in Fukien Province. The civil war in China forced the family to move once again, and Li went to work in a customs office in the coastal city of Amoy. She met the Amoy manager of the China and South Sea Bank, and was offered a job in the branch the bank was about to open in Hong Kong:

> *My official title was bank secretary, and I was responsible for all the English correspondence and telegrams of the bank . . . In this job I got to know foreign exchange bankers well. They would stop by the bank at eleven o'clock every morning. They were not used to seeing a woman bank officer, and at first they thought that I was hired as a decoration for the bank. But my boss told them that I was a better worker than some of the men.*

Li was introduced to her future husband by the elder brother of one of her schoolmates. They dated for six months before deciding to become engaged in the summer of 1935. She describes their weekend courting:

> *We agreed that Shu-pui should spend at the most ten dollars per weekend. On Saturdays he would work until seven o'clock in the evening. We would dine at a restaurant at eighty cents per person for a dish of rice with chicken and abalone on top, and then go to the Hong Kong Hotel Roof Garden to dance. The entrance fee was one dollar per person which would include one soft drink. On Sundays, Shu-pui would work until ten o'clock in the morning. We would go for a walk in the countryside, return home for a bath, then take lunch. After that we would either go to a movie for sixty cents per person or to a tea dance for one dollar, which would include cakes and sandwiches, and then home to dinner.*

They were married on 11 January 1936 at the Union Church. Her husband insisted she resign from the bank as his salary was sufficient to support them both. She was idle and bored and returned to her job within a month.

The Japanese occupation of China in 1937 brought a temporary halt to the civil war and sent a flood of refugees into Hong Kong.

> *We founded the Hong Kong Women's War Relief Fund Raising Association. We gathered money, medicine, medical supplies, and so on, and sent it to the front . . . It was difficult to get women to join at that time. I had to go personally to get them to join.*

In 1938, the manager of the bank recommended that Li should receive a promotion and pay rise. Upper management agreed to the promotion, but argued that she had married well and did not need the increased salary. Li soon resigned her position at the bank and began work as a full-time volunteer. The Association was re-established in 1938 as the Hong Kong Chinese Women's Club, of which she eventually became Chairman.

The Lis fled Hong Kong during the Japanese occupation, settling briefly in Macao, then in mainland China, where Dr Li practised medicine. After the war, they returned to Hong Kong, to take on two major challenges. One was the rebuilding of the Hong Kong Sanatorium and Hospital,

CONCUBINES

There were certain ways you could get a concubine. If your wife did not give you a son, if your wife did not respect your parents, or if she doesn't do what you want her to do . . . But these rules had been very much abused by the people in Canton, not because their wife did not have this virtue or that virtue, but just because they wanted a concubine. Some men had thirty or forty concubines. I have a friend here in Hong Kong who had thirty . . . Somewhere around thirty, not today, but at the time . . .

Ellen Li

which had been damaged during the occupation, the other was the raising of their three young children. Even this was not enough, however, for Ellen Li. She became involved in every aspect of women's rights, family planning, free education and the fight to abolish concubinage:

> *It made me angry. The women accepted it because they were quite poor. In Hong Kong, it was a way that people could make money. If the amah [maid servant] had a daughter she would teach her how to cook and sew, send her to school for a year or two and then sell her as a concubine . . . The child would help around the house and then when they got to be eighteen or nineteen they would sell them for $5,000 to be a concubine. The more concubines you had, the more status you had. The more you have the better, just like buying cars, you see . . .*

Her laugh is unrestrained and open. Many Chinese women, and certainly the older generations, are very restrained, and rarely express emotion spontaneously or openly. There is always a filter of reserve between the feelings they have, and the emotions they express. Her chief instrument in the struggle to end concubinage was the Chinese Women's Club:

> *The club was founded by me, so I had more or less control. I drafted the constitution. Whoever became a member had to be a wife, not a concubine, not a number two wife . . . Many concubines wanted to join for the status, but we didn't allow it . . . The men resented what I was doing. I had a lot of opposition. I had to do a lot of lobbying. I started a petition. I sent it to the government three times.*

Practical problems arose after the war, when people began to travel. In order to obtain a passport the legal status of your marriage had to be established. Some concubines held certificates of marriage, or contracts, from China, but many had lost their documents during the war. There were also increasing problems with the settling of estates, and establishing the legal status of the children of concubines. Pressure came not only from Ellen Li's organization, but from the basic legal impracticalities of this ancient custom in what was becoming an increasingly cosmopolitan

114

and wealthy city. This pressure resulted, in the late 1950s, in the government handing the problem to a senior member of the Legislative Council for consideration:

> *After reading the petition, he said he was very old-fashioned. He said we are bound by the charter of Captain Elliot. When Elliot occupied Hong Kong, he proclaimed that Chinese should be governed by Chinese tradition and law, not by British law, therefore we cannot change the situation. It killed the whole thing off . . . He was a very good friend of mine but still I got so upset . . . But in a few years' time he died off, so I started it off again . . .*

She speaks quickly and impatiently, someone whose mind is racing faster than words can follow. She sometimes confuses pronouns and says 'he' when she means 'she'. The Chinese language does not define masculine or feminine, it is always gender neutral.

Li was able to convince women of the necessity of changing the laws by arguing for the future security of their daughters and granddaughters. If they didn't outlaw the practice, and change the laws, their daughters and granddaughters could become its victims.

Finally, in 1971, the Legislative Council acted, and concubinage became bigamy and therefore illegal, after decades of struggle by Ellen Li and her allies.

Another achievement she speaks of with great pride was the establishment of equal pay for equal work:

> *I felt very strongly about it. Women were paid seventy per cent of what men got for the same work. It was just the accepted practice . . . It wasn't too hard to change that law because it had already begun in Britain. We followed many of the changes that happened in Britain . . . They did it in stages. So much each year. It took three years before we were on a par with men.*

The achievements of the early 1970s were temporarily overshadowed when Li was diagnosed with cancer in 1974, when she was sixty-two. She claims that the following ten years were the most fruitful years of her life:

> *I had decided to retire. And then I thought, if I retire, what am I going to do, sit at home moping and waiting to die? So I said, 'I'm going to give it ten more years. I am going to work very hard for ten years, and then that's it.'*

She continued to fight for the status of women, for better conditions for servants, medical care and education for women, all notable goals, but argues that the marriage law was her most important project:

> *In Hong Kong, women are given a lot of opportunity. You can be anything, but traditions die hard. I always say equality begins at home. If you don't treat your daughter equally, how can you expect others to?*

NO DOGS OR CHINESE

We saw discrimination in Shanghai, in the International Zone, where foreigners ruled. There were signs in the parks, 'No dogs or Chinese allowed . . .' It made me very, very angry. I thought one of these days, we are going to kick them out . . .

SHANGHAI AND HONG KONG

I found that the culture of Hong Kong was fifty years behind the times. I came from Shanghai, which in my time had always been ten years ahead of its time. Women had the vote. They had equal rights and there were already women in high offices. In Hong Kong no woman held a top post.

Ellen Li

Every Saturday afternoon, the Lis go to Pacific Place, a cavernous underground collection of hundreds of shops and miles of crowded passageways. It is their Saturday ritual. Dr Li buys *The Economist*, *Time* and a few London papers, and Mrs Li visits her favourite jewellery shop. They follow the same route and find themselves at an open café on an upper floor just in time for tea. We join them because Mrs Li wants to give us an updated list of her most important achievements, and legislation passed with her support. We take the opportunity to show her the result of her sitting with Lord Snowdon. She glances at it quickly and is clearly unhappy. She passes it to her husband. He examines it carefully. He admires it and says it is a good likeness and an interesting expression. Dr Li is a passionate amateur photographer himself. Mrs Li says with some disappointment that it shows her age. Her reaction is touching – vanity from a woman still filled with the pride and passion of youth.

As we get up to leave, she hands us an envelope containing a handwritten list of her most important personal firsts. She has underlined the four key ones in bright red ink. She was the first Chinese woman in Hong Kong appointed to the Urban Council (1964–9), and the first woman in Hong Kong appointed to the Legislative Council (1966–73), as well as the first Chinese woman in Hong Kong given an honorary degree LLD from the University of Hong Kong (1969), and the first woman in Hong Kong awarded a CBE, by Queen Elizabeth, in 1974.

ELSIE TU

A small white car pulls up to the hotel. The back door opens and out she steps. She is thin, and stands erect and tall. She is grandmotherly and proper. Her light blue eyes are fearless, and her gaze direct and unwavering. She seems to be seeing far into the distance, far past the people she meets, to the task at hand. This is not the sort of elderly woman one would offer a helping hand to unless she asked; everything about her declares a fierce independence.

Elsie Tu was born in England in 1913. She trained as a teacher and went to China with her first husband in 1947. She continues to teach and to fight for the rights of Hong Kong's poor and underprivileged. Her chauffeured car is a rare spot of luxury and privilege in a life of devotion, and is one of the perks of being a member of the Legislative Council. She is the only Caucasian photographed by Lord Snowdon for this book.

She asked if there was anything special she should wear for the sitting. We told her to wear what would make her most comfortable. The first thing she asked when she arrived for the sitting was if she had dressed 'appropriately'. She emphasized 'appropriately'. She meant had she dressed properly for Lord Snowdon, not for her photograph.

As we approached the studio, she allowed her excitement to show. This is a woman who has defied the triads and the British government. She was glowing; her eyes sparkled with excitement, like a little girl on her birthday being made the centre of attention by someone she admires.

Tu and Snowdon sat on the sofa outside the studio and talked. Snowdon's charm eased her fierce and feisty spirit. She reminded him that they had met very briefly in the 1960s, during an earlier trip he had made to the colony. She opened her purse and brought out a yellow, faded scrap of newspaper. 'There,' she said, pointing to a smudge in the corner, 'That's me.' Snowdon looked at the clipping, squinted and did his best to recall the occasion.

Tu claims it was her father who inspired her to work for the underprivileged. He had fought in World War I and had returned a changed man. He was largely self-educated and widely read and had

DON'T TRUST THE RICH

You know it is very difficult for any of us to know what those big businessmen are really like. They all came from China, and if they brought money with them, they were probably robbing the country. If they didn't bring money with them, they probably used some kind of illegal means to make it. So we don't really trust the rich.

Elsie Tu

ambitions to become a politician in Britain. He hoped his daughter would go to university and then enter politics. Tu disappointed him by deciding to become a missionary instead:

> *I think it was because I was feeling disillusioned, life seemed to be so empty, it was a dead end living in Britain. Mission work seemed to bring some light into my life.*

She had become a dedicated Christian in university and worked in the missionary field for ten years:

> *I had wanted to go to Africa, but I married a man who was interested in China . . . It wasn't what I thought. I was taught to convert the heathen, but the heathen converted me. I didn't turn to Buddhism, but I came to the conclusion we had a lot of cheek to think our religion was the right one, and everyone else's wrong.*

Tu was in Nanking when the Communist forces took the city in April 1949. Conditions had been bad and inflation crippling. She says they expected the worst from the Communists, but found them better behaved than the Nationalists under Chiang Kai-Shek:

> *All the missionaries decided to leave at the same time. We were going to go to Borneo, but when we got into Hong Kong we met some friends and they encouraged us to stay. That was 1951. I have been here ever since.*

Tu says the most striking feature of Hong Kong in those early days, when she was teaching, was the division between the Chinese and the British. She claims the gulf wasn't bridged until the 1970s. She has a very low regard for the wealthy and sees them as essentially corrupt:

> *They couldn't have become rich unless they had done something . . . The first thing I learned from my students was that money speaks, you can get anything with money . . . That is now breaking down. We are getting more people who have learned that corruption is bad. They are beginning to change their ideas and I think there is a lot of generosity in Hong Kong that wasn't there before.*

Tu continues to live and work among the Chinese in Kowloon. She says that it was the effect of corruption on the lives of the poor that spurred her into political activism. She doesn't care how such activities hurt the adults, but could not tolerate the sight of children orphaned or abandoned. It was hard, frustrating work to persuade the police to take the simplest action to protect the most helpless citizens:

> *I went to the police and said there were children being knocked down by speeding army trucks. They said, 'It was an army job, not a police job.' I went to the army and they said, 'It's a police job, not an army job.' I said I didn't care whose job it was, I wanted a sign put up to slow down the trucks so children wouldn't be killed. It took two years to get a sign put up!*

She used this incident as a platform to run for Municipal Council in 1963. In February of that year, just before the election, the government decided to level illegally constructed huts housing hundreds of poor:

> *It was the coldest February in a century. I was asked to go and see what had happened, what the government had done. They had flattened the huts and left the people in the cold. I*

PRESS FREEDOM

Freedom of the press belongs to those who own the press.

Elsie Tu

remember clearly seeing one old couple sitting on a bed and someone had kindly propped up a piece of iron in front of them to protect them from the cold. One woman tried to commit suicide by jumping off the hillside. I was furious . . . The land wasn't needed. The official at the housing department said they had no right to be there. I asked what he expected them to do, float in the air or float in the sea or what? He told me it was none of my business. I was in tears by this time . . . They finally agreed to let these poor people put their huts up on a place called the seventh cemetery. It was horrible for them, because they were always finding bones.

She is quite frank in declaring that the Governor at the time was, in her opinion, corrupt. But she says Hong Kong has benefited from three very fine recent Governors: MacLehose, Youde and Wilson. She is critical of Governor Patten and suspicious of his motives:

I think he is undoing all the good we have built . . . The great democrat, the future Prime Minister of Great Britain, I suppose . . . I just have my suspicions that he is just trying to make a name for himself. I hope he truly cares about Hong Kong, but can you think of any reason why a man who stood for election in Britain and lost would care about Hong Kong?

Could this be the same blushing schoolgirl at Snowdon's knee? She is energized by her anger and disgusted by what she sees as British ignorance and condescension. But part of her criticism of Patten's democratic reforms stems from her own frustrated attempts to promote democracy for Hong Kong:

In 1966, I went to London for six weeks. I lobbied all the MPs I could find to get more elected seats for Hong Kong. The answer was always no. I thought it would be a way to fight the injustices. They said nobody wants democracy in Hong Kong. They also said China wouldn't like it. Do you think China likes it today?

Tu sees the time leading up to 1997 as a dark period for Hong Kong. She feels the political squabbling over Patten's reforms and the damage to direct communication between Beijing and Hong Kong will eventually affect the economy, and jobs will be lost. Her fundamental concern is always for individual suffering.

It is hard to believe this is a woman in her eighties. She matches Emily Lau's passion and sometimes imprudent declarations. We ask her why she has worked so hard for others, and what, after all these years, her life in Hong Kong has been for:

You would understand if you came to my office and saw us rejoicing when we find a house for someone . . . It may be some simple thing like getting somebody public assistance or getting a larger flat for someone who is terribly overcrowded, or a flat for someone living in a hut . . . You would understand if you were there when one of these people travels a long, long way just to come and say thank you . . .

A Time of Progress

Things were pretty calm in the 1970s because Murray MacLehose came into government. He was Governor right through the seventies. One after another, he introduced exactly the things I had been asking for: education, social workers, more housing, legal aid, and curbs to corruption. He used to call me at home and ask me to give my advice, not just me, but other people. He used to ask how to deal with the crime situation, what can we do about corruption and so on? And he really worked hard. The seventies were a time of great progress socially.

Selective Deafness

Well, previous Governors have always talked to me, but this one, as soon as he found I didn't agree with him, he didn't want to talk to me. He doesn't want to hear it, he doesn't want to hear anybody who doesn't agree with him.

Elsie Tu

SALLY AW SIAN

We arrive at the offices of Sing Tao Newspapers, situated in the Hong Kong Club building, 3A Chater Road, Central. Sally Aw Sian is the heiress to the Tiger Balm fortune, and the Chief Executive of the largest circulation Chinese language newspaper with world-wide distribution, *Sing Tao*.

Aw Boon Haw developed the formula for the mentholated ointment called Tiger Balm in his kitchen in Burma. Tiger Balm was an instant success and is still sold all over the world. Aw spent his money well and extravagantly: he developed the Tiger Balm Gardens on Tai Hang Road in Hong Kong, and built huge homes in Singapore and Rangoon. He supported Chiang Kai-shek against the Communists, an error that led to blacklisting and the confiscation of his property in China. His name has only recently been rehabilitated.

Tiger Balm is no longer part of the family's holdings. *Sing Tao* was a minor part of her father's empire while he was alive, but has now grown into a huge conglomerate with holdings in real estate and printing plants, and with offices in every major city in the world. Her name may have got her in the door, but it is her genius, a powerfully concentrated mind, and forty years of hard work that has made *Sing Tao* into a billion-dollar business.

Sally Aw Sian was born in 1932. She has never married, and lived with her mother until her mother's death in 1994. It is highly unusual for a daughter to take over a family business. Sir Y. K. Pao's sons-in-law run Wheelock, and when Dr Li Shu-fan died without a male heir, control of the Hong Kong Sanatorium and Hospital passed to his brother, Dr Li Shu-pui; not his daughters.

When Sally Aw Sian enters the small office where we wait to do the interview, we assume she is a secretary. She dresses casually and enters quietly, almost cautiously. She seems very distant and cool and answers our questions sometimes defensively.

She would rather not discuss the family history. She wants to talk about the business she runs. She says that most published accounts

A WORLD NEWSPAPER

We are the only newspaper that goes around the world using the facsimile through satellite relay. We send pages directly from Hong Kong to Vancouver, and in turn from Vancouver to Toronto, New York and San Francisco. This is for the US and Canada. Now we are looking forward to having something similar to that for China, because we said we are the only paper that has world-wide publication, so why shouldn't we go to China – because we are a Chinese publication?

Sally Aw Sian

sensationalize her father's success. To correct the records, Aw Sian has recently commissioned a book on her family:

> *The project started quite a few years ago. We were going to start with the history of* Sing Tao *newspaper . . . but we can't get away from my father. China has rehabilitated my father's name so we have been able to get a lot of information out of the country. That's one of the reasons why I visited China . . . I did not want to be used by China. I was invited back to China because I am the representative of such a big media group . . . I didn't decide to go until they began returning all the properties. We have many properties in China that my father owned that they are now returning to us . . . They are doing that for everyone, except*

> *we got better terms . . . They gave us all the vacant possessions and they even whitewashed the buildings so that we don't have to spend money on them. You can do what you like. You want to rent it or renovate it, that's up to you.*

She says she has worked in the newspaper business for forty years:

> *The family owned the newspaper. I got in through the back door. It was the easy road, but you still had to prove yourself.*

She has always held managerial positions and never worked as a journalist. *Sing Tao* went public in the 1970s and after that the company undertook an aggressive expansion and diversification:

> *I felt just being a publisher was not going to be good enough, so we diversified quite a bit into all kind of things . . . We expanded all over the world. We bought real estate and then we had to back up a bit. We thought it would be better to spread ourselves around but if we bought real estate only in Hong Kong we would have had no problems at all.*

Sing Tao has since invested in printing plants on the mainland. We ask her about the problems of being a woman executive:

Sometimes being a woman actually gives you an advantage; if you are the only woman, you get all the attention and you attract a lot of attention.

We ask her if she has any concern about censorship of the newspaper after 1997:

I hope not. You never can tell . . . That's one of the reasons why we have started to publish in China, to educate them. We want them to understand that the country will only grow if the people have access to information.

Aw Sian is optimistic about Hong Kong's economy as it approaches 1997. She says she already has considerable investments in China and would put more in if her interests were not already so widespread internationally.

We returned to her offices some months later to show her the results of her sitting with Lord Snowdon. Snowdon had drawn out two very different characteristics. When Sally Aw Sian saw them she chose the photograph showing her engaged and in control. We disagreed with her choice. She struck us as cool and distant when we first met, but we soon realized that this was simply a very shy woman, and that we had been misled by our own preconceived notion that a successful chief executive must be cool, confident and aggressive.

Her secretaries had gathered around the photographs on the table in the small office. She wanted their opinion. They are comfortable with her, relaxed and direct in a way we never saw between male executives and their secretaries. They chose the gentler image, the shy smile and the quiet vulnerability. Sally Aw Sian was not at all dismayed by their choice, or ours, in fact she seemed flattered and touched that we had come to see her that way.

We met Sally Aw Sian one last time in Toronto, in autumn 1994. A reception was being held for Anson Chan on her first official visit to Canada as Chief Secretary. We heard her mother had died and we expressed our condolences. In spite of her loss, she seemed happy and relaxed, and she told us all about the new printing plant she had just opened that day in Toronto. She asked about our book, who was publishing it and where it was going to be printed. She said her company could do it, and could they bid on the job? We exchanged business cards. She looked up at us and smiled and said, 'It's just like Hong Kong, isn't it? . . . Always doing business . . .'

THE GOVERNOR'S PACKAGE

Chris Patten comes in as a different type of Governor because he is a politician. He does bring in quite a lot of new things by going straight to the public. I thought that was supposed to be very good. But he has used that to support his view, rather than being very frank like the politicians in the West, like in Toronto. I mean, they are very accessible. You can go and talk to anyone in Toronto, it's no big deal. Whereas here, previously, if you go to see the Governor it's really a big deal, because he wasn't accessible to you. Patten is showing he is accessible to the public, which is good, but not in the real sense. He is doing it because he wants to influence them for his cause. Chris Patten's package, that sort of thing.

Sally Aw Sian

MAGDALENA LEE

Magdalena Lee invited us to her home. She lives in a large apartment on Magazine Gap Road, on the same street as Martin Lee. She had just returned to Hong Kong from a visit to her factories in China. Her companies manufacture clothes for the American designers Calvin Klein and Ralph Lauren. Magdalena Lee built M. Magtague Company Limited after the death of her first husband, and she now employs over 1,300 people.

It is hard to believe that Lee was born in Canton in 1942. She looks like a woman in her mid-thirties and has the energy of a woman much younger. She was a little girl of seven when the Communists took Canton. Her father, a successful businessman, was away, and the invading troops tortured Lee and her mother, to seize his fortune. At one point, the mother was suspended in a tree, while the child, buried up to her neck, stared up at her. Lee tells the story in flat, unemotional tones:

> *My father was in Hong Kong in 1949 when the Communists came. He had left my mother and I and a household of servants to go attend to his business in Hong Kong. Whenever my mother ran out of money, she cashed in some of my father's gold. Everyone knew my father was quite rich. My father asked us to come out to Hong Kong. We left China but my mother didn't like Hong Kong and wanted to return . . . I remember it was 15 August in the Chinese calendar when the Communist soldiers came and took me from my bed to arrest me. They put me in a cell with a female journalist. And they began to torture me. They hung me up by the legs and by the toes trying to find out where the family gold was buried. But I really didn't know . . . They dug up the garden and ransacked our house, they looked everywhere. My mother was arrested and very badly tortured . . . They tied her up in a tree in a graveyard and buried me up to my neck . . . This sort of thing went on for three months.*

STARTING SMALL

I decided one day that I wanted to come home. My son was growing. So I left my job and came back to Hong Kong. With the little savings I had, I started an office with four sewing machines, a secretary and a driver.
Magdalena Lee

She was finally saved by a Russian colonel, a military advisor to the Chinese Communists, who took pity on her. Her mother was released the following month. The Communists held Lee and her mother under house arrest for the next four years. They forced Lee to write to her father in Hong Kong and have him send money back to China.

Eventually, her father was able to get in touch with a high-ranking official on the mainland, and purchase visas. Lee and her mother escaped to Macao, and the family was reunited in Hong Kong.

Lee's father enrolled her in Lingnan school, which proved too much of a cultural shock. She spoke no English and felt alienated from her classmates.

> *My father said, 'I'll give you two choices, either you go to England to school or you have to be married.' The thought of marriage frightened me, so I said I would go to England to study. Unfortunately, after two years, my father was found to have liver cancer and so I returned to Hong Kong.*

Lee and her mother lived well for a few years on her father's estate. She continued her education at a Canadian convent school. Lee had wanted to go on to university but instead went to work for British Airways for two years, during which time she met her late husband. They were married in 1966. They had been married six months and Lee was five months pregnant when it was discovered that her husband was terminally ill. He lived only long enough to enjoy his new son's first year of life:

> *My father-in-law offered me a job at the family bank. He said he would pay me well and if I stayed twenty years I could then turn the position over to my son. But I could not stand the idea of having him as a benefactor. I want to be paid for what I contribute. I don't want charity.*

Within a year she was hired by an American company in the fashion industry and quickly became a successful buyer. She left her son with her mother and went to study the fashion business in New York. Lee spent two and a half years in New York before moving to Europe for three years.

She finally returned to Hong Kong to start her own company. Her old boss from New York came to Hong Kong on business and took her out to dinner:

> *He said, 'There is a person I want you to meet, and you have to change the business you're in.' I said, 'Who is this person?' and he said, 'Calvin Klein.' They were looking for someone in Hong Kong to work for them.*

Lee met Calvin Klein and his partner, Barry Schwartz, in Europe. They asked her to make 200 dozen cashmere sweaters for them and if she did well, they would give her their sweater business. She did, and they did, and, in 1976, Lee bought her first factory. She now has factories in Hong Kong, and Hangzhou and Shenzhen in China:

> *Hong Kong has become extremely expensive. Our business is extremely competitive. So in order to maintain and continue my business I have to explore other areas where I can manufacture with much cheaper labour.*

DESPERATION

The Communists made me go through poverty and helplessness. And that feeling of desperation has made me feel that if I were able, I will never let myself go through that again.

Magdalena Lee

What do her friends make of her success?

> *I have the financial independence they don't have. But they know I have paid a big price for it. I don't have a family as they do. When there is trouble I must weather it myself.*

She speaks passionately about her desire to raise her son to be independent and strong. Lee sent him away to school in England when he was twelve, so he would receive the attention and discipline she was unable to provide because of her busy career. She wrote to him – always in Chinese – and encouraged him to do well in his education:

> *I must admit that of all the things I have ever done, the investment I have made in my son has returned the greatest rewards.*

He has completed an undergraduate degree in the United States and hopes to enter Harvard Business School.

> *I asked my son two questions when he graduated from university. First, I asked if he regretted not growing up with a father. Second, did he feel deprived as a child because his mother was so busy with her business . . . He said he certainly missed having a father, but he said I had never let him feel neglected – either for not having a father, or because his mother was so busy.*

SELINA CHOW

Her voice is high and insistent, and her eyes warm and friendly. It is a seductive combination of contrast, the warm eyes and the sharp tongue. Selina Chow is one of the highest-profile and vocal members of the Legislative Council. She trained in the theatre and worked in broadcasting. The perfect preparation for a political career.

Her father was born in Canton in 1900 and came to Hong Kong at an early age. Chow was born in 1945 and is the only child of one of her father's three wives. The wives lived separately from each other, and Chow grew up feeling quite alone and isolated. She says her father always encouraged his children to get a good education:

> *My father had two sisters. One became a doctor and the other became a lecturer at Hong Kong University. They were about his age but he supported them through university. In those days, girls were not supposed to get much education, so it was quite a progressive thing for him to do.*

She stresses again and again that her father went to great lengths to be fair. When questioned on her feelings about her father having three wives, she argues that for a man of his generation it was common practice, and a sign of wealth and social status. But it created problems:

> *I never talked with my half-brothers and sisters. We sort of avoided one another. But I felt that our father wanted us to communicate. When I went to the UK, I was given my half-sister's telephone number. But she didn't want to see me. Obviously, there must have been jealousy between the mothers and the way to resolve it was to pretend that the other ones didn't exist . . . My father wanted his children to come together and behave like brothers and sisters. And in fact that did happen when he had a serious stroke . . .*

She says that the children found that they all shared the same deep respect for their father.

Chow went to the University of Hong Kong and then went to London to study Drama. She also admits going to London because her future husband, Joseph, was completing a degree in Engineering there.

> *I was always quite artistically oriented. I sang and danced. And my parents were very interested in the performing arts. They were also very interested in the Peking Opera . . . My*

CHINA IS NOT ALWAYS WRONG

Some of the politicians like Martin Lee and Emily Lau believe they are always right, and China is always wrong. They refuse to see things from the Chinese point of view. Now I am not saying that we as Hong Kong people and political leaders should see things from the Chinese point of view and agree with them all the time. I am saying you have to understand their point of view in order to persuade them to the rightness of your thinking.

Selina Chow

mother used to take lessons two or three times a week. I can still remember as a kid coming home from school at lunch to spend about half an hour singing Peking Opera because that was when my mother had her lesson.

Chow went to the Wilkes Booth College of Speech and Drama in Kent. But it was exposure to a different culture that affected her the most. She found the atmosphere freer than the stuffy colonialism of Hong Kong in the 1960s. She says it was her first taste of real democracy:

There were certain things in Hong Kong that were taboo. You musn't talk about China, you musn't speak of China and Taiwan together, and you had to be careful not to criticize the government.

Her father wrote to her in London and told her a new television station was opening up in Hong Kong. He felt there would be exciting opportunities for someone with her talents. She was hired immediately at Television Broadcasts (TVB), and did both on and off camera work:

When I first started at TVB, I was working thirteen-hour days, seven days a week. This was in the late 1960s . . . It was a very exciting time. Everybody was working very hard to put out the best, and you felt you could try anything.

She progressed rapidly through the ranks, and by the time she left in 1977 she was Assistant General Manager:

The reason I left was that I was at the peak of my career. I was churning out all these soap operas, which were getting ninety-five per cent of the audience. It was becoming harder and harder to keep up the record . . . I also began to feel discrimination for the first time. The first ten years I didn't feel it, or I just brushed it aside and went on doing what I felt had to be done . . . But then I started to see men receive promotions that should have come to me.

Chow says it made her very angry, so she left TVB and started a production company that she ran successfully for ten years. It was during the early years of this new business that the government approached her to serve on the Urban Council:

ASKING QUESTIONS

I think that Hong Kong has changed a lot in the last twenty years. I think that Governor MacLehose started it, because he allowed dissension. He felt that you needed the right balance of civil servants and people like myself. People who were young professionals. People who were prepared to question and were not afraid.

Selina Chow

It was quite important, because the Urban Council was actually making all the decisions for the cultural and recreational activities in the urban area around Hong Kong.

It was not long before her effectiveness was noted. She was appointed to the Legislative Council in 1981 and has served continually since.

She is concerned that the political squabbling over Governor Patten's reforms has distracted people from the real question of the nature of the government, and the Chief Executive after 1997. It is a question that troubles her deeply. Her voice is sharp and sends words out like arrows; she raises her arms and punctuates the air with her hands.

131

We feel that the Chief Executive should have a popular mandate, but the Basic Law says that the Chief Executive will be chosen by an electoral college. The Chinese are trying to exact some kind of control over the choice of Chief Executive . . . What they are afraid of is that they would have someone who would aim to bring down the Chinese government from that position!

But Chow does not believe that the British should be taking such a confrontational stance with China:

Accusations don't build bridges of communication. What we need to do is a very basic job of persuasion and explanation. We want to keep Hong Kong as close to what it is today as possible, economically, socially and politically.

When Ellen Li says something she considers important, contentious or confrontational, she

tucks in her chin and settles deep into her chair – as if preparing for a gale-force wind of disdain. Elsie Tu sticks out her chin and dares. Sally Aw Sian couches her contention in corporate prose, and seeming indifference. And Magdalena Lee stares down the transgressor with a cool, firmly fixed gaze that is both fearsome and seductive. But Chow conducts the ebb and flow of conversation as if leading an orchestra through a troubling patch of atonality.

Chow and Snowdon seemed to hit it off immediately, they spoke the same language of imagery, allusion and metaphor. She was ready to have fun and enjoy the experience of being photographed by him.

The final images were puzzling. Snowdon had caught the animated Chow in freeze-frame. But the portraits seemed to be about something more specific. She faces the camera squarely, but seems to be marking or framing some space between her and Snowdon with her hands. Or is this an elaborate dance from the Peking Operas of her childhood? Snowdon asked her what her best feature was and she told him her hands. He said, 'Show me.' And so she did.

FEEDING THE SENSES:

WORK TO LIVE, OR LIVE TO WORK?

ARE YOU MARRIED, OR DO YOU LIVE IN KOWLOON?
An English matron, c. 1920

Kowloon held all the amusements and temptations a single man might want. There were brothels and opium dens and gambling houses. Married men were expected to amuse themselves at Happy Valley racecourse on Hong Kong Island, and to socialize with the Establishment at the Hong Kong Jockey Club, founded in 1884. Today, there are two racecourses in Hong Kong: Happy Valley, on the island, and Sha Tin, which opened in the New Territories just north of Kowloon in 1978.

However, the people of Hong Kong still play as hard as they work. And if they have money, they play big. Larry Yung, the head of the Beijing government's investment firm, CITIC, recently won almost US $5 million accidently, on a bet he placed on his mobile phone. He explained that the horses that won were not the horses he thought he had chosen; he read the series of numbers incorrectly from a list he had prepared and they turned out to be the winners. He donated most of his winnings to charity. This seems a staggering amount of money to have won, and an equally impressive amount to risk, but it reached the papers only because of the fluke of winning the way he did, not because of the size of the purse.

Happy Valley racecourse attracts 50,000 fans every Wednesday and Saturday between September and June. The betting turnover for each race day can exceed US $100 million.

Gambling brings together luck, fate and entrepreneurial nerve. It is also accessible and affordable to the whole population. In the off-season, or for those in need of a more regular fix, there are Stanley Ho's casinos in Macao, a forty-minute boat ride away.

The earliest recorded horse race occurred in Hong Kong in 1845; the first meet held at Happy Valley took place in 1846. This is the jewel in the crown, and one of the most beautiful

興於詩立於禮成於樂

*The Odes stimulate
the mind, the Rules of
Propriety build the
character, and through
music one becomes
accomplished.*

and modern racecourses in the world. It is located on some of the only flat land on the island, and is where early settlers first lived. It was also a swamp, and malaria and other insect-born diseases soon forced settlers to move. The land was eventually drained and a racecourse constructed.

The Li family hospital, with its luxury suite overlooking the present racecourse, began as a TB sanatorium near the site of a fire at the racecourse in 1918, which killed six hundred people. At that time the stands were constructed of bamboo bound together with twine – the same materials used today to fasten together scaffolding on the exterior of buildings under construction. The stands were packed for the annual Chinese New Year's race. Some of the families were preparing meals over small fires or kerosene stoves under the shelter of the stands. Those sitting overhead watching the races jumped up and down excitedly and the stands collapsed, trapping hundreds, and the kerosene stoves soon ignited the bamboo and twine. Heavy winds quickly blew the flames into an inferno. There is no danger of a repetition of that tragedy today: every modern safety precaution and device is in place.

The Royal Hong Kong Jockey Club controls all the racing and betting in the territory. It is a non-profit organization and donates surplus funds to charitable and community projects. Almost US $250 million was allocated to charities and cultural projects in the year 1992–3. Much of the money goes to high profile projects such as the Hong Kong Academy for the Performing Arts, but it is also possible to come across a small community clinic on Lantau Island built with Jockey Club funds.

As with everything in Hong Kong, there are layers and layers in the gambling industry, which is a combination of sport, entertainment, and fundraiser for social and cultural pursuits. As elsewhere, gambling helps those who have disposable money to dispose of it while trying to earn more of it. Nearly all Chinese love gambling, but here it seems to be almost a natural extension of the entrepreneurial spirit, and requires many of the same qualities – daring, resilience and, yes, luck – that have propelled so many entrepreneurs up the ladder to the penthouse.

The invitations were delivered by hand to our hotel. It was the first race of the new year and our first chance to view one of the most beautiful racecourses in the world. We were invited to join Mr and Mrs Li Fook Wo, with friends and family, in the Honorary Steward's box. Li Fook Wo is the Chairman of the board of the Bank of East Asia. The Bank of East Asia was founded in 1919 and has more branches in China than any other foreign bank. The Shanghai branch has been at the same location since 1927 and has 155 employees. It is profitable enough to support all the other branches in China. Normally, Mr Li refuses requests for interviews, but we were able to interview him for this book because his daughter and son-in-law are Torontonians, and friends.

The occasion turned out to be something of a Canadian reunion as there were several couples from Toronto in the Steward's box that night. Many overseas Chinese return to Hong Kong to spend Christmas and New Years with parents and grandparents.

The envelope bearing the invitation also contained a light green paper badge that would allow us access to the exclusive private boxes on the upper floors overlooking the racecourse. There was also a piece of paper in the envelope with the numbers one to six listed down the margin, and a series of numbers typed out beside each number. Mr Li, a great horseman, had been on the telephone to fellow owners and trainers and prepared a list of the best bets on each of the six races to be held that night. Mrs Li, a tall, elegant woman, is also passionate about horses, and recounted how, as a small girl, she had been taught to ride by a White Russian colonel in Shanghai.

It felt more like being on a great ocean liner than in a private box at a racecourse. It was one large room perhaps fifteen feet deep and thirty feet long with a balcony offering an astonishing view of the track. Two large round tables were set up for dinner. The women would all sit at one table and the men at the other. Side tables were quickly filling up with plates of Chinese and Western delicacies. There were at least four waiters serving, and attending to our drinks.

When we walked out onto the balcony, it seemed more like a movie set spread out before us than a sporting event. Happy Valley racecourse nestles between hills and a forest of high-rise apartment buildings. The reflecting walls of concrete, sloping hills and low clouds concentrates the other-worldly lighting and the roar of the crowd. A huge new colour television screen had recently been installed in the centre of the track to show close-ups of the horses as they rounded far corners.

Our balcony connected to others; privacy was assured by a low fixed partition. Some in our party raised glasses hello, or nodded acknowledgement to acquaintances on adjacent balconies. It was all very civilized, and the decorum not much changed from earlier times.

Our attention was drawn to the sea of bodies down at the edge of the track. We were told that all the serious betting action came from there. Wagers from the private boxes above contributed very little to the gross receipts.

We were asked to place our bets as we were about to be served the first course of a six-course meal. We passed on the betting. But others rushed out into the hall to the betting windows. The evening would unfold in this order: place your bets, sit down for a bite, then get up in time to watch the race, and begin again. And while we were cheering our horses on, the waiters would clear the tables for the next course.

We were asked to guess the winner of the fifth race. No one had been having much luck on the selection Mr Li had provided. We felt the number 6 horse lucky, a horse called Echo. Not lucky enough for us to bet on ourselves, but a worthy choice for others. Some actually took our advice. And to our amazement the number 6 horse won. There was now one race left to run. Everyone wanted to know which horse we favoured. Again, we felt number 6 lucky. And this time we put money on it ourselves – HK $20 to win.

Our hearts were in our mouths before the horses were even at the post. Quite a rush for only $20. Number 6 shot out in front and led the race most of the way. But rounding the last corner he began to fade – or the others began to catch up – it was hard to tell, and he finished third. It was not losing our $20 that distressed us, but how we had let down our hosts. We only hoped they had not wagered too much. But they were returning with fistfuls of dollars. They appreciated our tip, but bet to place, not win. This is Hong Kong, where serious gamblers always hedge their bets.

In this chapter, then, we are going to look at individuals who have drawn their fortunes from the disposable income of their fellow citizens. Stanley Ho is the casino king of Macao; Sir Run Run Shaw brought cinema and television to the territories; Solomon Lee's fortune springs from Po Chai pills, a herbal medicine popular with Chinese throughout the world; Joyce Ma is the doyenne of high fashion and a retailing genius; and Frank Chao made his fortune in shipping, but spends it in interesting and extravagant ways – singing in karaoke bars late into the night, and owning a stable of thoroughbreds that would be the envy of a Saudi Prince.

STANLEY HO

Stanley Ho's offices are on the 39th floor of the Shun Tak Centre, 200 Connaught Road, Central. If he is here, there will be a stretch cherry-red Rolls-Royce Limousine parked at the kerb, near the lifts, on the ground level of the sheltered drive reserved for taxis and limousines. The limousine was there, and in spite of rush-hour cross-harbour traffic we had arrived in time for our 4pm appointment. The guards who greeted us on the 39th floor wore uniforms, and the security cameras were obvious, trained on every corner of the elegantly decorated waiting room.

The stage was set. This is the headquarters of the casino king, a man known for his extravagant lifestyle, and legendary courage – or nerve.

His assistant, Helen Hung, led us into an enormous boardroom and explained that Dr Ho – the title reflects an honorary, not a medical degree – had been delayed by business in Macao. She said he had just left Macao by helicopter and should be in the office in fifteen or twenty minutes. She told us to make ourselves comfortable and sent for Chinese tea.

This is the top floor of the Shun Tak Centre. We look down into Victoria Harbour and the Macao ferry docks that brought Stanley Ho his fortune. Through floor-to-ceiling windows we can see all of Kowloon, and early construction of the bridge that will connect Lantau Island and the new airport to the Kowloon waterfront. Reclamation on both sides of the harbour constricts water traffic to a crawl. The hydrofoil ferry to Macao moves away from the dock slowly, and only speeds up and takes flight when well free of the congested channel.

A helicopter approaches from the northwest. There is a landing pad on the roof of the ferry docks directly beneath us. The helicopter lands and a tall, thin man steps out. He disappears down a flight of stairs at the edge of the roof. The helicopter's engine roars, it lifts off and swings out over the channel, tracing the route of the most recent ferry to Macao. We wait.

When we are ushered into the office, it is to discover Ho already in place, and apparently hard at work. He has been whisked from the helicopter pad through an unseen entrance into his inner sanctum, in a little bit of the stagecraft we have come to expect of Hong Kong's mighty. We are expected to be impressed. We are.

This is the most beautiful and impressive office of any we have seen, perhaps twenty feet wide by forty feet long, and dominated by a huge window along the north wall, ten feet high, floor to ceiling, and

A DEGREE OF CORRUPTION

Corruption? The whole world is corrupt. It's only a matter of degree.

Stanley Ho

affording a magnificent view of Victoria Harbour. The glass in this window is held in place by steel frames, six feet wide; six of them are ranged along the wall, and sitting on pedestals before each frame are enormous jade or stone carvings of dragons or Chinese junks. The sculptures seem to float out over the harbour, enacting a legendary scene of ancient times.

We are standing at the door in the western wall, Dr Ho faces us at his desk against the eastern wall. He heard the door open, he knows who we are and why we are here. He does not look up from his work, not immediately. As Helen Hung approaches his desk, he starts and looks up as if surprised by intruders. She is so far away we cannot hear what she says to him. He gets up, and moves towards us. He shakes our hands and motions us to sit at a round conference table. His suit is beautifully tailored. The most interesting feature is that the sleeves of his jacket have been ironed to create a crease that runs down the length of the sleeve from his elbow to his wrist. This is a very old-fashioned way of pressing a suit. It is often an unwelcome surprise to foreigners when they send suits to be cleaned in even the best hotels. To a Westerner, the first impression is that a mistake has been made.

Ho asked for a list of questions to be sent in advance. He has prepared his responses to these questions, and refers to them for the first half-hour of the interview.

His English is impeccable. His eyes are unforgettable, they have a cool and predatory ferocity.

Stanley Ho was born into a wealthy and famous family in Hong Kong in 1921. His great uncle was Sir Robert Ho Tung, 1862–1956, who had been chief comprador at Jardines, and had made his first million by the turn of the century:

> *I started from riches to rags, and then rags to riches . . . When I was thirteen my mother suddenly said to me, 'Sorry, Stanley, I can't support you any more. Your father's gone bust and has left the colony for Saigon . . .' My father was comprador and director of Sassoons.*

There were five Ho brothers. Three were compradors at Jardines, one a comprador at the Hongkong and Shanghai Bank, and another at the Mercantile Bank. Ho explained that all five brothers went in together to speculate on Jardines shares, but the shares plummeted, and they were all wiped out:

> *My uncle shot himself. Another uncle also committed suicide. My father was not so brave, he left home . . . My mother said unless I got a scholarship I couldn't carry on in school. I won't say I was a bad student, but I wasn't a very good one. You know, when you are rich you are spoiled. But I worked hard and every year I got a scholarship until I got into Hong Kong University . . . I was in my third year, with one more year to go to graduation. I was in the Science Faculty. Then the Pacific War broke out and the Japanese came and started bombing Hong Kong.*

WORK HARD OR STARVE

The success of Hong Kong is that we don't give so much welfare, social welfare. You will not like to hear this from Stanley Ho. The system is such that you work hard or you starve, as simple as that. The weak, the old people will get a little help. The rest work hard. Friday, you want something done, tomorrow, Sunday, everybody will be working. That's our success. Very little social welfare. And we don't need to spend so much money for defence. You see, a tax haven and all the money comes in. A little bit of trouble in Shenzhen yesterday, more money comes in. Some trouble in the Philippines, money will come. Thailand, money will come . . .

Stanley Ho

Ho fled to Macao, the Portuguese colony on the Pearl River just forty miles west of Hong Kong, on a small junk, with ten dollars. One of his uncles lived in Macao, as did Sir Robert Ho Tung. Ho says it never crossed his mind to look up Sir Robert, but his uncle had offered him a job as a chemist while he was still at university. Ho went to work at the Macao Cooperative Company, which bartered surplus equipment from the Macao government for food from the Japanese:

> *I became a director and shareholder of the company within one year. They found me so useful in my negotiations with the Japanese and with the government. I became a partner of the company . . . And I could speak Japanese. I made my first million in that same year . . . You know in war, there are lots of opportunities. If you are hard-working, and if people trust you, you can get a lot of material from them on a loan basis. You don't have to pay them immediately . . . I started because of my knowledge of chemistry. I bought a lot of chemicals . . . I became a millionaire at the age of twenty.*

Ho soon moved the rest of his family to Macao, where they stayed until the end of the war. The work he was doing was dangerous, and, on more than one occasion, almost cost him his life:

> *I was often sent on a boat into free China to buy oil. The Japanese needed a lot of oil . . . the pirates came, they shot two of us, a sailor and the pilot. They machine-gunned the boat. I tried to hide. They caught me and stripped me and one of the pirates took the money I had . . . The others kept asking for money. I told them one of the pirates had taken it. They asked if I could identify the pirate. I said yes. I pointed him out. They all went for him and began fighting for the money . . . their junk started to drift away. I told the engineer to start the engine. The pirates had destroyed two of the engines but there was another one, a hidden one. The crew were all frightened; they thought the pirates would kill us. But, when the engine suddenly started, the pirates all jumped overboard, and we escaped . . . It was very, very dangerous.*

Ho returned to Hong Kong at the end of the war and set up an import-export business. He prospered throughout the 1950s but says the real turning point came in 1961, when the

141

> ## FREE ENOUGH
>
> **Unlike other places around us, our taxation is a tax heaven,**
>
> **a maximum rate of 16.5 per cent. Where else on earth can you get that?**
>
> **And still we have freedom. We don't need so much human rights, or**
>
> **democracy, we're free enough. Free enough.**
>
> *Stanley Ho*

government in Macao asked for a tender of the gambling franchise. He eventually won the franchise and opened his first casino in 1962:

> *The key was my knowledge of Hong Kong. Hong Kong in those days was booming. Very prosperous. Macao was a dying city. Macao had been a paradise for three years, but once the war was over that was it . . . I said the way to save Macao was to bring it closer to Hong Kong. I promised to introduce high-speed boats. In those days it took four hours to get to Macao. I also promised to dredge the channel to the inner harbour, the harbour at Macao was always congested because of the channel. Nobody believed me. They said the outer harbour would silt up in a week. I also promised to clear the outer harbour of squatters. There were about one thousand squatters in boats. There were many obstacles, but I succeeded. They even threatened my life. And they said we will send two hundred beggars to stand outside your casino. The old concessionaire said he would threaten all the croupiers so they would not come and work for me. He said no one would have the courage to lease any premises to me. But I had lived in Macao for three years and eight months during the war. I knew everybody, and I knew they were all bluffing.*

There was a knock on the door. We were interrupted by a senior executive needing Stanley Ho's signature. It was past six but the day far from over. The executive apologized for the interruption and placed the document carefully in front of Ho, who took a fountain pen from his inside breast pocket, uncapped it, held it in his hand like a surgical instrument, and then signed the blank space above the black line with an elaborate scrawl. He looked at the signature for a moment and then signed the page again, to the right of his signature, but this time with Chinese characters.

The first three years of the casino business were difficult. The early customers were almost exclusively Portuguese; the Chinese only came slowly. We asked how he survived those early years:

> *Not easily, really not easily . . . But you see, luckily, I was already a multi-millionaire in Hong Kong real estate. My partner was Henry Fok, who was very wealthy, so we managed to survive . . . It really started to take off about 1965. We had more business because we had introduced more high-speed boats, the jet foils . . . Everything was going well until the Cultural Revolution . . .*

Ho says that Macao was soon overrun by demonstrators carrying red flags and waving banners bearing the thoughts of Chairman Mao:

> *It was like a Communist territory. At one point, I had to close the casino down for two*

months. No use, what's the point, there was no business to keep it going . . . And worst of all, the squatters returned – refugees from China.

However, Ho resumed business with China in 1970, when the worst of the Cultural Revolution had passed. He bought and sold finished goods and materials. And the casino kept on, making steady but modest profits. Then, the business entered a boom period in the early 1980s, largely due to the computerization of the Hong Kong government, and the issuing of identity cards, which made it faster and simpler for people to travel to Macao. But will Beijing allow this to continue after China takes back Macao from the Portuguese in 1999?

The Communist leaders came to Macao and had a talk with me about gambling in the future. I said to them, 'Let's be pragmatic.' Macao will never survive without gambling. It does not have a good harbour or an airport. Hong Kong is already a financial centre. What attractions can Macao provide? I told Lu Ping that the governors said, 'Stanley Ho, we mustn't rely on your gambling tax. We must diversify. Let's think of industry, tourism.' Not a single one of the governors could do anything. I said, 'I think when the Special Administrative Region government comes in, it will be the same.' Macao is only five square miles. Where can you have big industries? And speaking of tourism, I said, 'I think I have done the most for you already.' When I first came to Macao there were fifty thousand tourists coming to visit, and today we have seven million.

He believes that the Chinese treat him fairly in large part because of his business ties, and the investments he has made on the mainland. We wonder if China won't make substantial changes to Hong Kong after 1997:

They don't dare, because they know once they do they will upset things, and then Hong Kong will not be Hong Kong any more . . . They need Hong Kong, both politically and financially. They need it politically because their final objective is not Hong Kong, or Macao, it's Taiwan. First Hong Kong in 1997, then Macao in 1999, and then Taiwan . . .

Stanley Ho arrived early for his sitting with Lord Snowdon. He ate lunch by himself in the Chinese restaurant in the Royal Garden Hotel. The cherry-red Rolls-Royce waited in the drive. He looked relaxed and confident. Ho has a reputation as a skilled ballroom dancer, and a man who loves to stand up in front of a crowd and speak. He is a showman, a man of the theatre, and the casino king. Snowdon had him put on an Issey Miyake shirt and jacket. He did not complain, he enjoyed the charade. The jacket was not a perfect fit and was pinned at the back of the neck and at the shoulders. Stanley Ho came out of the dressing room and modelled his costume for us before going into the studio. He moved stiffly, not wanting to dislodge the pins at the back of his neck.

Snowdon was pleased with the portrait. Ho looks like a mandarin, inscrutable, wise and powerful, with eyes that penetrate like daggers.

JOYCE MA

Joyce Ma was born into a wealthy family of merchants in Shanghai in 1940. Her maiden name is Kwok, and her grandfather and his brothers built the Wing On department stores. Wing On is Chinese for 'forever peace'. The family chartered a plane and fled Shanghai in 1948. Ma remembers the family compound in Shanghai with its two huge homes joined together and called the white house, and beautiful gardens and a private lake. The family flew to Hong Kong where they stayed for three years before moving on to Australia for another three years. They finally returned to Hong Kong in 1953:

> *When we came back my father started at the bank. Then I got married. Oh, I am jumping around because I think that part of my life is so . . . How I see life is like a movie . . . everything that happens in one's life is not by accident, it is meant to be . . . Don't you agree?*

She speaks softly and listens very carefully. She sips a cup of tea. She holds the cup with both hands like a delicate flower, raising it to her mouth as if holding a fragile scent. She smiles like a child, with her whole face:

> *When I graduated from school I was supposed to go abroad to study. I had already met the man who was to become my husband and preferred to take a secretarial course here just to be near him. After I finished the secretarial course, I also took an etiquette course. It was what was expected.*

Ma did some modelling and studied Italian. She speaks both French and Italian, and reminds us again that this was obvious preparation for her future career in the fashion industry:

> *I got married when I was twenty-one. I had my first daughter when I was twenty-two, and then eighteen months later my second daughter. And then my uncle came to me and asked if I would like to go to work in his department store. He wanted me to open a small boutique. It was a dilapidated old store. I didn't know anything about business . . . We learned by mistakes, but it was a great success right from the beginning.*

COMMODITIES, NOT FEELINGS

Here in Hong Kong the purpose is to acquire a commodity, and that is all. They don't dare to look at their own feelings. They don't want to, they ignore it. They don't want to express it. This is how they were brought up and this is how it is . . . If their material gain were to be taken from them, they would be so lost.

Joyce Ma

It was a tiny shop, only 350 square feet, but her timing was perfect. It was the early 1960s, and Hong Kong's new rich had begun to travel. They had developed a taste for the clothes they had seen in London and Paris, and were eager to buy closer to home:

I was soon given another small area of 220 square feet, and then we added accessories, and later got into men's clothes. And when the new department store in Central was ready, they gave me the entire floor, which was 3–4,000 square feet.

Ma soon began organizing fashion shows and imported English, French and Italian designers:

I was the first one to bring an English choreographer with English models to Hong Kong to give fashion shows, in the late 1960s. It was at that time that we brought in couturiers like Lanvin, Jean Patou, Valentino and Yves St Laurent.

The management of the store complained she wasn't selling enough:

I ran to my husband and I said, 'I resigned, what do I do, I won't be able to travel any more?' He said, 'Let's see if we can start up a business of your own and see if someone will back us.' He said if I found the shop space he would go out and find backers. I came back after two hours and said, 'I've found it!'

She rented space in the Mandarin Hotel, and her husband registered the new company as Joyce Boutique:

I had been quite devastated after I left the department store, but after a few days everything had been solved and I was on a plane again on my way to Italy to look for new Italian designers to represent.

The shop was only 850 square feet, but it was an immediate success. Ma explains that there had been a fire in the shop before she moved in, and that the Chinese believe that a fire consumes all the evil, and only good remains:

It was in a corner of the Mandarin Hotel. The women would go to lunch or tea in the Clipper Lounge and then come in and shop. We had a desk and sofa, and they would come and use the telephone to do their Stock Exchange business.

In the early 1970s, Ma was one of the first to appreciate the new Italian designers like Armani, Versace and Valentino:

I was not as fluent in Italian as I am now, but it served the purpose. Everyone was just starting. They were not like now. They were not grand. They were very happy to even get their first orders. This is how I started with Armani . . . Later, it was quite another matter, and they wouldn't talk to you at all. I remember in Florence and Milan. They were in their heyday. They had a booth in the Palazzo Piti and it was crowded with people. They wouldn't allow anyone in. I just stood by the door and waited. I was very persistent. I just sat there and I said, 'I am not leaving – you can switch off all the lights, but I won't leave until you talk to me . . .'

PINNING FOR YOU

Some of my clients from then are still some of my clients now. They still joke with me, 'Joyce, do you remember the time when you were on your knees pinning up my dress?' If you want, I can go on my knees again and I can pin for you.

Joyce Ma

Competitors soon appeared in Hong Kong and she lost Valentino and Versace. In order to keep Armani, she had to dedicate her 850 square feet exclusively to him. In her second year of business she opened another shop in the Peninsula Hotel, and then opened a shop selling decorative furniture and objects:

> *It was much too early, and it was also a very small shop. Some decorators bought from me but most would rather spend US $800 on clothing for their social life, than have a beautiful table for their home. I had to close that shop.*

That shop, and an early venture into Taipei, are the only failures she can recall:

> *I am just very blessed, what can I say? . . . I have never really had to look into that other side of the business, of course I know it, but I never had to worry where the money was coming from, because my husband looked after that part of it. I was just on the creative side, and because the business was always expanding and successful it was never an issue.*

International designers became big business in the 1980s. They all wanted shops of their own; they didn't want to be sold with other designers. Ma hit upon the idea of grouping a series of small, separate shops together, the culmination of which is her Joyce Galleria in the Landmark Building in Central:

> *A valuable business in the fashion industry is even shorter-lived than the trends . . . You have to always keep up, because business is never that great. People don't normally buy very much. Every few months you have to make critical decisions. You put all your eggs in one basket every six or eight months. You have to be very instinctive.*

In the early days, Ma was known to have a short fuse and an explosive temper. But today she has changed:

> *Four years ago I was introduced to meditation. Ever since then it has been my way of life. Once you meet your spiritual master you recognize it . . . Since I have always had everything, and life has been great for me, what else is there? . . . One wants to look into the meaning of life, and what one can do in return.*

When we ask her if this inward search has changed her views on Hong Kong, she falls silent. We wonder if she senses a coming crisis of some kind:

> *I hope not. The crisis doesn't necessarily have to come with let's say an abrupt stop in material gains. Many of them have to look at their marriage, their children, what they are, and whether they want to live that way. I think this is when they would want to look at themselves. It is not only the material side, if there is going to be a market crash. I think they have to look into their own lives. Life cannot be smooth sailing all the time, although having so much helps . . . But it is not only what you have, it's what you see . . .*

SIR RUN RUN SHAW

Sir Run Run Shaw was born in Shanghai in 1907. He moved to Singapore in 1927 with his late elder brother, Tan Sri Runme Shaw, and together they created a film distribution business for Chinese language movies. The brothers moved to Hong Kong in 1959 and built Shaw Brothers Studios. Today, Shaw Brothers accommodates the production facilities of Television Broadcasts Limited, or TVB, of which Sir Run Run is Executive Chairman. TVB is the largest supplier or library of Chinese language programming in the world.

We conducted the interview at the studios on Clear Water Bay Road in Kowloon. The building sits on the edge of a hill and seems much smaller than its reputation would suggest. We notice a stable of Rolls-Royces at the bottom of the driveway that leads up to the studio. There are perhaps fifteen Rolls of different years, models and colours parked side by side, under the protection of what looks like a very flimsy tin roof. They look as if they have not been driven in a very long time. Some are covered in a fine layer of dust. The studio itself looks much as it must have when it was first built. There is an odd shabbiness to the place. It is dispiriting. And then we watch a very beautiful young woman, the very definition of a starlet, walk out the front door and down the hill towards us. She smiles as she passes. She stands by the road and waits for her ride. We are reminded that this is the movie business, where everything is illusion, and nothing permanent. Nothing, except Sir Run Run Shaw.

We wait for him in a large room with shag-pile carpet that seems to be brown. The furniture is green or blue, it is difficult to be sure as the lighting is very bad. There are pale squares on the wall where paintings have been moved, or taken down. Finally, he enters. He is thin, almost frail, with bright intelligent eyes and a smile forced out of primly pursed lips. A burly assistant shadows him. Sir Run Run motions for us to sit, then sinks down on a sofa at right angles to ours, while his assistant settles at the far end:

When I went to Singapore I started with one cinema in 1937. By 1939 I had 139 theatres . . . All these theatres showed films from America . . . Our own pictures were not good enough. So that was the idea – why

HELPING OUT

I think if people can, they should help out. China is so backward, schools in China are so backward. I think it is important. With education we can understand the world and improve it. Once people are educated, they can contribute to society.

Sir Run Run Shaw

don't we make movies in Hong Kong, and make high quality pictures? That's why I came to Hong Kong, to make movies. Also, China was not politically stable and labour costs in Singapore were very high. It was fifty per cent cheaper to make films here. And of course there were plenty of Chinese here.

The family had other business in Singapore, as well as investments in property and banks. But taxes in Singapore were fifty per cent, and only fifteen per cent in Hong Kong:

It was not very easy, because the industry was very young. We started with nothing. We sent a lot of money from Singapore to acquire the land to develop the studio . . . When I first started this studio, I couldn't get anyone good enough – cameramen, make-up men, lighting, directors, artists. We started everything from scratch. We used to bring in people from America, Europe, Japan and Australia. In their contract it said they had to teach our people. They could go home at the end of three years. The Chinese are hard-working and willing to learn. In three years, most of them picked up on how to do everything.

He is nostalgic about those early days, and the constant struggle to improve the quality of the films he made:

Slowly, we built very expensive sets. In those days, if we wanted a table, we would hire a number of expert carvers to make it. It was real . . . Today, it's done by plastic mould. You want a palace, you just use plastic and paint with gold . . . A star in those days we paid $1,000 or $2,000 a month. Big stars got $2,000 a month. Today, some of the stars, they are asking US $1 million per picture.

At its peak, Shaw Brothers was turning out forty-four films a year; today they release only six annually. But quantity had as much to do with cost and expectation as anything.

A film in those early days might cost the studio $10,000 to make, and bring in close to $600,000 from its Guangzhou release alone. Shaw claims that quality was the most important aspect of the business:

When I saw a picture that was not good, I said, 'Throw it away. We don't want it.' We'd start all over again.

Shaw says that his business is as affected as any in difficult economic times. When people have money, they go to the movies; if they're broke, they stay at home. He says he could distribute his films in China if he wanted, but that there is not enough money in it yet to make it worthwhile. Shaw has sent hundreds of millions of dollars into the mainland over the past decade, to build schools and hospitals. TVB was Shaw's brainchild, and brought television to Hong Kong:

BREATHING
This kind of exercise is very old in China. This breathing exercise, when we practise this exercise, the blood circulates in your body better and you have better health. I am eighty-six, and I am quite normal, I can talk to you, I can work, I can eat, and everything else . . .
Sir Run Run Shaw

Before I got into the TV business, there was rediffusion in Hong Kong. You paid $10 a month and you could get four pictures a day on your TV. But bad sound and fuzzy pictures. Then I thought, if TV is so popular in other parts of the world, why not in Hong Kong? So we got a few friends together and started television. Overnight, rediffusion was out . . . Now you have satellite coming, and pay TV . . . Pay TV is like rediffusion all over again.

Patience was never Shaw's greatest virtue, a point that was driven home when he arrived early for his sitting with Lord Snowdon and immediately announced that he could only stay for twenty minutes. He was in a foul mood. Even Snowdon's considerable charm proved ineffective. Snowdon explained patiently the problem with the white shirt and tie. Shaw stared back as if he were a madman. Snowdon calmly moved on to discuss the glasses. Shaw was speechless. Finally, as the minutes ticked by, Snowdon ushered Sir Run Run into the studio and shut the door. We listened, but could hear nothing.

By some miracle of will, Snowdon managed to get Shaw to remove

ENOUGH COOKS

You have the school, the polytechnic. Today you want anything you tell the polytechnic. I want somebody who knows how to cook for my hotel. Six months later they will produce for you one dozen cooks.

Sir Run Run Shaw

his glasses. But Shaw warned that he also wanted photos with his glasses on. And Snowdon had him cup his face in his hands to hide the shirt and tie. Only Snowdon knows how this was accomplished. It was a battle of formidable wills. Would Shaw flee? Could Snowdon get whatever it was he wanted? Yes. And a gentle, vulnerable, whimsical old soul is the image that remains – not in memory, but on the printed page.

Snowdon claims his portrayal of Sir Run Run is the best portrait. He said he knew he'd got it. He could feel it. He then thanked Sir Run Run for his patience. Shaw looked up and reminded him he was also to take some pictures with his glasses on. Snowdon said he was very sorry, but his twenty minutes were up.

GET ON

I am a businessman. I do business. Politics I don't understand much. How many seats in the Legislative Council, all too complicated. What I want, is leave us alone, let us get on.

Sir Run Run Shaw

SOLOMON LEE

The Mercedes-Benz is the most popular car in Hong Kong. It is considered reliable and luxurious. It is also the car most likely to be stolen. Mainland pirates power high-speed boats down the coast; they co-ordinate their arrival so that the stolen car arrives at the waterfront when they do. The car is quickly loaded on the boat and the boat roars back to China with its prize.

Solomon Lee buys a new powder-blue Rolls-Royce every few years. The government levies a sales tax of one hundred per cent on cars, so a Rolls-Royce can end up costing US $300,000.

We asked Lee if he wasn't concerned that his Rolls would be stolen and shipped off to China, along with the Mercedes-Benz. He shrugged and said they weren't stealing Rolls-Royces yet, because they didn't have enough spare parts on hand to fix them. He thinks it will be five years before they will start stealing Rolls-Royces for the mainland market.

Solomon Lee was born in Guangzhou in 1936. The family moved the headquarters of their herbal medicine business to Hong Kong following the Japanese invasion of 1937. Lee comes from a family of thirteen children, all from the same mother, with nine of the children still alive today. Lee's company makes Po Chai pills, small brown pellets of Chinese herbal medicine sold around the world:

> *My grandmother had a dream one night and in the dream a Chinese God gave her the formula. That was more than one hundred years ago. The company was only registered in 1900. But we were doing business in China long before 1900: it was only in 1900 that you had to register your business.*

The firm started in a small village not far from Canton. The pills are made from ten ingredients:

> *In the old days they used a big pan and they rolled the pills in powder. You have a small granule, and you roll it over and over in the powder and it gets bigger and bigger. You add one layer of powder and then another. In the old days, there might be fifty layers of coating.*

A REFLECTION

Here, the money we make we keep.

Solomon Lee

The medicine was not an immediate success. But there was a flood in the Lees' village, and everyone fell ill. The family distributed their medicine and everyone's health improved. The legend spread and the family opened a factory in Guangzhou.

HONG KONG IS BEST

How can I go to another place to set up a factory?
Hong Kong is the best place to do it. The taxation is low, and the raw
materials are close by. Let's say I move to another country. That means
I have to ship all the raw materials from China to that factory. And then
the taxation is much higher than in Hong Kong.

Solomon Lee

The business continued with difficulty during the Japanese occupation of Hong Kong. The raw materials came from China, and obtaining permits for shipping to Hong Kong was difficult.

Lee completed a degree in Business Administration at the Chinese University of Hong Kong. His father let the children decide their own careers. Lee's father became heavily involved in the real estate market in Hong Kong in the late 1950s and early 1960s, and Lee took advantage of this opportunity to fill his father's position at the head of the Po Chai company in 1961.

Lee brought new technology into the factory and used advertising to open up overseas markets. Production is now ten times what it was in 1961. Po Chai pills can be found in Chinatowns all over the world. The greatest technical innovation came with the development of their own pill-making machine:

I had to look for a granulating machine all over the world. Most of the machines could not grind the herbs. Some of the herbs are oily, some are hard, and some have very tough fibres. So we copied some details from a foreign machine, and modified it for our production here.

Lee is ambiguous about 1997. On one hand, he worries about the control he might lose over his business, on the other, he sees the China market as a huge opportunity:

I am not encouraging my children to come into the business. They won't graduate until 1998. But there will be a fourth generation. There are my brothers and sisters and cousins. It's very complicated. I think they should make their own choices.

Lee competed for Hong Kong at the Olympic Games in Montreal in 1976 and Los Angeles in 1984, in pistol shooting.

When I was young my elder brother taught me to shoot. I found that I had a talent for it. The first time I competed for Hong Kong was at the Commonwealth Games in New Zealand in 1974. Because it was my first try I didn't do very well. Then I got a gold medal in the Commonwealth Games in 1982. I'm the first Asian to have won a gold medal in pistol shooting in the history of the Commonwealth Games. I think I'm still the only one.

FRANK CHAO

Frank Chao was born in Shanghai in 1934. The family fled to Hong Kong in 1948:

We had a lot of land in China, buildings and houses. But the only thing we brought to Hong Kong was half a ship . . . My father owned half a ship, his partner the other half . . . A ship is a natural floating asset, so we brought the only asset we could with us.

Chao came into the family shipping business after obtaining degrees in Marine Engineering and Naval Architecture. He returned to Hong Kong from university in 1961:

At that time, the company was not so big. Over the years it has grown into a big company. We have approximately sixty big ships including container ships. In total, we have about 130 ships.

The 1960s were boom times for the shipping industry, and Japanese shipbuilding made it easy to acquire enormous fleets:

At that time, if you had a ship built in a Japanese shipyard, financed by Japanese companies and chartered to Japan, you could get eighty per cent of your financing from the Japanese. So when you built a ship, you only needed twenty per cent of the money. Assuming a ship in those days cost US $3 million, you only needed $600,000. Also, payment was made in four stages. The first stage was to sign the contract, the next stage was when you started building the ship. The third stage was when the ship was all ready to go in the water, and the fourth stage was when the ship was ready to be turned over to you. So, initially you only had to pay out five per cent. Assuming again that the price was US $3 million, you only needed to find something like US $150,000 in order to sign a contract.

This made building a huge fleet relatively easy in the 1960s. The recession of the early 1970s, and the oil crisis, rendered many of the ships idle, and almost ruined some of the largest shipping companies. When business came back, three giants remained:

156

CHINA GAINED AT TIANANMEN SQUARE

Looking back, even looking at Tiananmen Square, the situation, I would say, maybe lots of people don't agree with me, but China came out of the Tiananmen Square incident well. Because of Tiananmen Square, it triggered off Eastern European freedom. After that there was a merger between East and West Germany, and termination of the animosity of Russia against the States.

Frank Chao

We calculate that there are approximately 300,000 people working in the shipping industry and related industries in Hong Kong. Fundamentally, shipping is controlled by three major Shanghai families. One is Y. K. Pao, another is C. Y. Tung. He passed away about five years ago and his empire is now run by his sons, C. H. Tung and C. C. Tung. Then there's Wah Kwong, the company started by my father, and run by myself and by my younger brother, George. So these are the three most important shipping companies in Hong Kong, and all are Shanghainese. The Paos are more concentrated on tankers, the Tungs are concentrating on liners and the container business, and we concentrate on dry cargo. Dry cargo means coal, iron ore, logs. Tankers are oil, and containers carry container boxes. There are three families and we each have our own speciality.

158

Chao points to 1985 and 1986 as another critical period for the shipping business. The Chaos were forced to do a financial restructuring by their creditors in 1986, and the Tungs were forced to do the same in 1987. At the time, the Chao family had the largest private collection of Oriental art in the world. Much of it was sold to help retire company debt. But much remains, and the penthouse floor of the head office on Hennessy Road in Wanchai is filled with jade and ivory carvings as well as an enormous mural his mother bought at auction for US $2 million. The restructuring took ten difficult months to complete. Public trading of the company's shares resumed in 1988. When it began, shares in Wah Kwong shipping sold for 10 cents; today they trade at about $12.

Chao speaks with great energy and animation. It is more a lecture than a conversation as he talks about China:

Up until 1978, I never invested any money in China because I had absolutely no confidence about the economic development of China. Fortunately, after Mao died, China started to change. 1978 was the year when everything started to change. Then you had Tiananmen Square and people worried about China. But, fortunately, this is all over. Today, I have great confidence in China.

When we ask him about the current squabbles between Beijing and the new Governor, or about Deng's successor, he shrugs and says that it is all a political game. He remains ultimately optimistic, but will not make predictions.

Chao brings the same quality of attention to his Oriental art collection and his stable of thirty

THE FABRIC OF HISTORY

**I think that Hong Kong without the textile industry
would not be the Hong Kong of today. Because the textile industry was
able to export and make money, and employ labour, this was the
beginning of Hong Kong. Today, maybe it is not as important, but in the
1950s and the 1960s, the textile industry was the most important industry
contributing to Hong Kong's prosperity.**

Frank Chao

thoroughbreds as he does to his business interests. In many ways, he sees them as all the same, and only really interesting when put into play.

He took up riding while at university in England and has been a member of the Royal Hong Kong Jockey Club for over twenty-five years. He is also Vice-President of the Hong Kong Racehorse Owners Association:

> *My wife still thinks I spend too much time and money on my horses but now that she has seen the first of my foals soon after they were born, she has become really interested in my horses. She also enjoys naming them for me.*

We never expected any of our subjects to show the kind of enthusiasm Frank Chao did for his sitting with Lord Snowdon. He arrived early, and brought with him two deep navy-blue *cheung sams*. They are traditional Chinese garments, a short one with separate jacket and pants, and a long one like a robe. They were beautifully tailored, and of a rich brocaded fabric. Chao said it is almost impossible to find tailors capable of such fine work today.

He changed quickly and joined Snowdon in the studio. An assistant was pressing the other *cheung sam*, as Snowdon wanted shots of Chao in both styles. Suddenly, we heard singing. Snowdon had asked Chao what he did with his spare time – if he had any. Chao showed him. He sang his favourite karaoke number, *Mona Lisa*, and danced.

159

HONG KONG MAN

HONG KONG HAS BECOME AN INTERNATIONAL, COSMOPOLITAN CENTRE, FOR FINANCE, FOR TRADE AND FOR OTHER THINGS. AND THE HONG KONG PEOPLE ARE NOT WHAT THEY WERE IN 1941. THEN, THEY WERE REFUGEES, OR PEOPLE IN TRANSIT, PLUS, OF COURSE, THE BRITISH. VERY, VERY FEW OF THEM IDENTIFIED WITH HONG KONG, OR SAW HONG KONG AS HAVING ANY IDENTITY AT ALL. NOR COULD THEY IDENTIFY WITH CHINA. THEY DIDN'T LIKE CHINA, THEY DIDN'T LIKE COMMUNISM, ALTHOUGH THEIR SENTIMENTS WERE ENTIRELY CHINESE. BUT WE ARE SO MUCH STRONGER NOW, BECAUSE THERE IS A WHOLE GENERATION OF PEOPLE WHO NOW REALLY IDENTIFY THEMSELVES AS HONG KONG MAN.

Wang Gung-wu

While this book is about the movers and shakers of Hong Kong, the issues raised are universal – the trade-off between individual responsibility and collective action; the argument, centred on what will happen with the Basic Law, about the rule of law; the conflict between political policy and the needs of business, between state control and entrepreneurship. Hong Kong is, in this light, a metaphor for what is going on all over the world, perfectly captured in the 'one country, two systems' argument. You will recall that this is the approach promised for the area for at least the next fifty years; that Hong Kong would continue to exist, within the bosom of the Chinese state, but following at least some of the precepts of capitalism, some of the tenets of democracy.

Easier said than done. There is an inherent contradiction between the freedom of choice

When you meet someone superior try to equal him; when you meet someone inferior look inwards and examine yourself.

that fires the entrepreneur to exploit markets wherever they exist, and the restrictions imposed by an authoritarian state. The contradiction exists in Boston, as well as Beijing, in Victoria, British Columbia, as well as in Victoria, Hong Kong; but here, it is exaggerated, highlighted, made manifest by the lessons of history and the lesions of modern life. In most of the industrial world, the gap is bridged by the untidy compromises of politics. Bold entrepreneurs are encouraged to launch their ventures with the nods and becks and wreathed smiles – to say nothing of the tax breaks and grants – of their host governments. But, at the same time, if they ignore the regulations these same governments impose to safeguard the nation, the environment and the market, they will be punished.

The rules are drawn up by the process of elective politics, which everyone curses, and everyone needs; government by complaining consent.

There is no such thing in China, where democracy is just another contagious virus, likely to prove fatal to the body politic. The regulations are made behind closed doors, and just as rapidly changed, so that what was commendable today is culpable tomorrow, and the only fixed rule to follow is that the gang in charge will tolerate no backchat. And yet, and yet. China must have the energy, the ideas and the hard cash that the regrettably wicked and demonstrably unruly entrepreneurs are spinning out here, on her own border, within her spreading skirt. It is no wonder the Chinese cannot decide whether Hong Kong is an opportunity or an infestation, and the people of Hong Kong wonder whether they are about to be enfolded or embalmed.

You can hear these issues vibrating through the voices on these pages. Many of the business figures we interviewed had some of the same contempt for the untidiness of democracy that bounces off the walls in the Forbidden Palace. But they understand, or at least the wisest of them do, that freedom of choice is not a negotiable commodity, that the open market brings with it the open mouths of critics.

It is far from clear that the rulers of China recognize the strange and contradictory creature with which they are dealing. They may well believe – certainly their tribal elders believed – that they can, so to speak, have their Hong Kong and eat it, too; they can keep the entrepreneurial and business skills of this place harnessed between the shafts of ideology. If this is the approach taken after 1997, nothing but tragedy lies ahead.

The three main parties to the arrangement – China, Britain and the people of Hong Kong – have been working away at these issues for years, but, with the deadline fast approaching, they are far from resolved.

There are two other complicating factors, one negative, one positive. Hong Kong is, in large part, the stamping ground of the most gifted of the Chinese who rejected China; something they can never forget, and the Chinese may never forgive. It introduces a certain testiness into negotiations over the future, in Beijing, and a certain nervousness over the results, in Hong Kong. On the other hand, there is a new generation moving up, both in the colony and in councils of government in mainland China. The drums of history may be moving off, out of hearing range, as the young technocrats now emerging from China's own evolving educational process come to deal with the new phenomenon cited by Wang Gung-wu, in the quotation at the top of this chapter.

The majority of the people profiled in this book were born in China, but have spent most of their adult lives in Hong Kong. Their identities are coloured by the insecurity such dislocation imbeds in the psyche, an insecurity that has driven some to remarkable heights. Today, more than fifty per cent of the population was born and raised in Hong Kong. This new generation has only known the triumphs and minor tribulations of post-war Hong Kong, and their insecurities, or the engine that drives them, has more to do with identity and culture, than privation and war.

A discussion of the forces shaping these people would not be complete without examining the role place has played in defining their lives. Place is more than the specific attributes of a particular landscape, it is about the quality of the light, the range of the climate, and the nature of the relationship between one neighbour and another. Place is about total environment, everything the senses take in.

Hong Kong is obviously more than the barren rocky island described in nineteenth-century documents. There are ferocious typhoons and torrential rains. Clothing soaks through with perspiration in the summer months, and only mad dogs and Englishmen go out in the midday sun (fewer of each these days).

The Peak, and cross-harbour travel, define Hong Kong for commuters and ambitious entrepreneurs. The Peak represents wealth and power, the closer the summit the clearer the achievement. Address reflects status: Central, the mid-levels, and the Peak. Much of Hong Kong's work force lives in the New Territories and must cross the narrow strip of water from Kowloon to Hong Kong Island each day. It is a daily reminder of Hong Kong's literal and metaphorical separation from the mainland. It is a journey that is now made easy by a cross-harbour tunnel; another tunnel is under construction. At the current rate of land reclamation neither may soon be necessary. These elements are unambiguous symbols reinforcing Hong Kong's purpose and history – tenuous links to unseen forces, and the frantic scramble up the ladder of success to the glorious heights above. This may or may not change after 1 July 1997. In all likelihood, those gazing across the straight will look just as enviously at the prize waiting at the summit of the Peak.

Most of the people in this book have carved out a space for themselves, an office or a home that reflects something of their character. They can afford to. The Harilela palace, Martin Lee's office, or the impeccable sobriety of Li Ka-shing's corporate lair. The individuals in this chapter are primarily artists and intellectuals. They live a life of the mind. They are not confined by space, but by the limits of their imagination. Their working spaces are wherever they happen to be.

We interviewed Wang Gung-wu in his Vice-Chancellor's office at the University of Hong Kong. We climbed up Pokfulam Road towards the Peak, and walked one last steep incline to the Knowles Building in the centre of the campus. We spent several hours in the Vice-Chancellor's office in a sea of ideas. It was the same with Charles Kao: ideas defined place. We interviewed Nansun Shi and Tsui Hark in the lobby of the New World Hotel – all glass and marble and business-class banality. And Raymond Wu? We interviewed him on the run, as he drove us through the busy streets of Kowloon to find a pharmacy to fill a prescription, in a quiet corner during a cocktail party, or before and after his sitting with Snowdon. This is what place means to Hong Kong Man: anywhere ideas have a few quiet moments to grow.

163

WANG GUNG-WU

Professor Wang Gung-wu is the Vice-Chancellor of the University of Hong Kong. He is an historian whose many books and articles have focused on the question of the Chinese diaspora. Wang has written about the famines, floods and wars that have driven the Chinese from China to every part of the world in search of a better future. Today, these immigrants, or the descendants of these immigrants, number sixty million world-wide. Many have kept close contact with their ancestral villages, and have financed schools and hospitals in the provinces their families fled so long ago. Much of the money financing China's current modernization comes from the pockets of these overseas Chinese. Loyalty and affection for the homeland is great, no matter how long or painful the separation.

Wang is of the diaspora. He was born in 1930 in Malaysia, and spent the eighteen years prior to his appointment to the University of Hong Kong in Australia. He is an academic and historian, but says that his position and responsibilities are closer to high government office than to university administration. He says that there are advantages and disadvantages to this higher profile:

> *On the one hand, people have great expectations of what you are supposed to do. On the other hand it gives me easy access to people . . . If I have a problem, I can go and talk to people very directly, and that is a great help. It makes life much easier. But the expectations mean that I need to get involved in many more things than a vice-chancellor normally gets involved in. Very quickly I was drawn into the government . . . Here I found myself really involved in governmental affairs, government committees of one kind or another, and then into the Executive Council for two years and nine months.*

The University of Hong Kong was founded in 1911. Today, ten thousand students are enrolled at the university:

> *Everything that happens here is related to my interests as an historian of China, as an historian of the Chinese overseas, as an historian of Southeast Asia, these are the three main areas of my professional*

THE NETWORK

In China, there is no democracy, so people look to their families. The only way you can do things is with connections, the network of relatives, because you don't have any other organizations to represent you.

Wang Gung-wu

164

A VERY FALSE IMAGE

The vast majority of the people in China have a very superficial
image of Hong Kong. It is something like the image of Shanghai in the
past. Pearl of the Orient. Parties. People. That kind of picture which is
quite false in many ways. Either that, or there may also be a picture of a
very materialistic, business-like people who just think about money all the
time, and having a good time. That sort of image. A very false image and
it's very superficial. No understanding at all. The people who understand
Hong Kong are the people nearest to us. I think the Guangzhou people
and the Shenzhen people. The Pearl River Delta. They have
a very good idea of Hong Kong life.

Wang Gung-wu

*interest. Almost everything that happens in Hong Kong hinges on all three. So in that sense I
am continually being stimulated, stirred to think about things, given thoughts which
influence my understanding of the subject. I am learning every moment.*

It seems appropriate that an historian be in such a privileged position in Hong Kong, able to
observe developments first hand. Wang is also very sensitive to the way the present will affect
the way he sees and writes about the past. He describes 1997 as the termination of a treaty, and
the end of a period of history shaped by misunderstanding. He believes, however, that Hong
Kong would have been taken back if the Nationalists had won the civil war:

*The Communists didn't take it back because they found themselves faced with the problem of
Taiwan on one front, and the Korean War on the other . . . And they knew they would need a
window to the West . . . They wanted to be left alone to develop their own Socialist society
free from intervention. At the same time, they didn't want to be entirely cut off.*

DIFFERENT HISTORIES

My deepest interest is in historiography. It's the way people
write history. I have always been fascinated by this, ever since
I was a student. I have always been fascinated by the fact that people
in different countries and different civilizations write history differently.
History is not a subject like science, that two plus two is equal to four.
It's not. History is written in different ways, perceived differently; how
you understand it, how you know it, how you gather information varies
from time to time as well as place to place.

Wang Gung-wu

The Hong Kong we know today was built in the forty years following the Chinese Communist triumph of 1949. The children of the refugee founders, born and raised in the colony, have raised the stakes; they have given greater value to the place by identifying themselves as Hong Kong people. The danger is that China may refuse to acknowledge something as distinct as Hong Kong Man. China may decide to see them as refugees of China, with no right to a separate identity:

The difficult part, and this is the fascinating part, is that there is ambiguity to Hong Kong Man . . . In speech, in writing, in the media, Hong Kong people are continually commenting on what is happening in China in a very free and uninhibited way. And that freedom of expression is powerful, and so valuable to Hong Kong, it is part of the Hong Kong identity.

And they want that freedom protected by a legal system that allows them the right as Chinese to care for China and tell the Chinese what's wrong. Tell them what to do. That, of course, creates a tension because the Chinese are saying, well, we are prepared to let you be, but don't dare tell us what to do. Don't contaminate us with your ideas . . . That creates tension.

But Hong Kong will only be different for a very short period of time. Already, Shenzhen, Guangzhou, much of the Pearl River Delta and Guangdong Province, have absorbed many of Hong Kong's characteristics. That exchange or absorption will only increase after 1997, and the fact that the whole region speaks a dialect (Cantonese) different from the Mandarin spoken in Beijing, suggests that censure would be applied to the region, and not exclusively to Hong Kong:

On the cultural side, the differences are not that great. I mean the people in Guangzhou could appreciate the same sort of joke, same sort of film, the same sort of novels written and produced in Hong Kong. And you bring a Cantonese from Guangzhou, and someone from Hong Kong together, and they understand each other perfectly. Not only because of the language, they know what it is all about because they already have a very good idea about Hong Kong.

NO FUNDAMENTAL CHANGE

There should be no significant fundamental change.
It should basically be roughly the same. There would be complications
here and there. And over time, there may develop some difficulties, but
the essential structures will remain. The nature of the Hong Kong
government, the legal system, the education system, the cultural values,
the religious freedoms, the freedom of the press and so on and so forth are
theoretically a part of the Agreement and are stressed in the Basic Law.
If those agreements are kept to, then there should be
no change. No, nothing fundamental.

Wang Gung-wu

We asked Wang how historians in China view Hong Kong:

Historians are not free to write what they think in China, especially not on modern history. They can do what they like about very traditional, old history, but contemporary history is highly politicized in China; under the Communist system, that's the way it has to be. And unless you analyse in Marxist, Leninist, Maoist terms, you really can't get yourself published . . . We have a choice, freedom of choice, but an historian in China does not have that freedom of choice. If he does not write along the accepted lines, he will not write again.

Wang has a large head, wears heavy glasses, and uses his hands to shape phrases in the air in front of him. He speaks with a hybrid accent, not quite Australian, not British, nor mid-Atlantic. He rounds his vowels and softens his words, so that his speech is easy to listen to. And, unlike most Chinese, he uses his eyebrows expressively to underline the importance of something he is saying, or register surprise at something he has heard:

When I am speaking Chinese, I think in Chinese. My sentences come out differently because the thought processes are different. My wife says and other people confirm that my behaviour is different. But I am not conscious of it. The body language changes, too, when I am talking to an audience of Chinese. Without realizing it, as I speak my body language seems to be affected. When I am speaking in English again, my body language changes and goes another way.

He reminds us that most Western universities are middle-class or bourgeois institutions. Hong Kong's universities, which began as elitist institutions, today are working-class. Parents with means have always sent their children overseas, and as Hong Kong prospered, the exodus increased. This made room for poorer children. The government made scholarships available to those with the academic qualifications but insufficient financial means:

NO ENGLISH

The vast majority of our students are from parents who do not speak a word of English, and whose contacts with English are extremely limited, and who studied English only for examination and not for any other purpose. Some have never met someone who spoke English in their entire life.

Wang Gung-wu

We have now become a really working-class university, much more so than in the Socialist countries or the Communist world. Even in Australia, the universities are middle-class. The working class in Australia have difficulty going to university.

Wang talks about Hong Kong embracing a strictly capitalist philosophy, even more than in the past, where faith is placed on survival of the fittest and natural selection through market forces. He says that this is the philosophy that survived the Cold War and that the Socialist approach seems to have failed:

We have people shouting triumphantly about the success of Capitalism over Communism. In the short term, they are right. In the short term, Communism failed. But of the broader philosophy of Socialism, to say that the caring welfare state is gone . . . Well I think the jury is still out on that . . . In the end, neither pure Capitalism, nor pure Socialism deserves to succeed, because they both have major problems. In the end, I believe that you have to take the middle road. It is all a matter of balance.

UNPREDICTABLE HONG KONG

I can put myself in the shoes of an historian in the 1930s and probably would have made, or drawn, wrong conclusions about the future of Hong Kong. But I would also say that almost everybody would have been wrong about Hong Kong. Nobody could have predicted the future of Hong Kong to be what it is today. Nobody.

Wang Gung-wu

We return to Confucianism, and the way of the mean. Wang has told us that his body language changes to accommodate his spoken language. What he feels deeply is reflected in his gesture. There is no tension in his body when he speaks of the search for balance, no gestures to help describe abstract phrases; he is sure, calm and comfortable. This is not a philosophy he has come to through study. This springs from the core of his being, and is as clear and light as air:

169

Actually, Hong Kong is a caring state, when we look at how the philanthropists subscribe to charities. Whatever their motives is unimportant. The thing is, they are subscribing. They are giving as well as taking. Maybe they are taking more than they give, but it is a matter of balance. You may say that a lot of people are greedy and money-conscious and take more than they give, but I would say that there are so many examples of giving that I find extraordinary in a society like this.

THE PAST IS PROLOGUE

I've always believed that my understanding of history is helped by my understanding of the present. That the past cannot be understood without looking at the present, just as much as I believe that the present cannot be understood without reference to the past. I mean I believe that the present can only be explained if you understand the past. I am influenced by what I live through, what I know of the present gives me insight into my understanding of the past.

Wang Gung-wu

CHARLES KAO

Dr Charles Kao is the Vice-Chancellor of the Chinese University of Hong Kong. He was born in Shanghai in 1933, and grew up there during the Japanese occupation. He remembers being forced to study Japanese in school. The family left Shanghai in 1948 and settled in Hong Kong. He studied at St Joseph's College and then completed a degree in Electrical Engineering at what is now Greenwich University in London.

We are interviewing Dr Kao in his office; one wall is almost entirely window and offers a view of a campus, that straddles several small hills in the New Territories.

Kao speaks quietly, almost tentatively and has a round, gentle face. His tone is even, his voice soft, and he displays little emotion. He is not a philosopher, his ideas and opinions relate more to his own experience than to a broader landscape. He is a scientist, more comfortable with cause and effect than with abstract concepts.

After completing his Engineering degree, Kao worked as a research scientist for a telecommunications company. He worked with microwaves and then switched to optics:

HONG KONG PEOPLE

I think Hong Kong people, after fifty years, have acquired a characteristic about them. Hong Kong people are highly pragmatic and very adaptable. You can say they are opportunistic, they are a very powerful group of energetic people willing to do anything and do it very quickly.

Charles Kao

Circumstances and luck were on my side as my boss was a very fine thinker. He suggested we work on a way to guide the optical wave . . . This was the beginning of the development of fibre optics . . . I consulted lots of experts about reducing transmission loss in transparent materials like glass and plastic. They all said it was impossible. I learned that when experts say something is impossible one should pay attention, because they rarely know what they are talking about . . . I gathered together a team of four people, and in 1966 we published a paper which caught the attention of some important people in the field . . . I spent the next twenty years bringing that research idea to a product. That was one of the most satisfying parts of my working life. I had the pleasure of getting an idea and seeing it actually become commercial . . . All our predictions were correct. Initially, there were many difficulties, it took a long time to get people interested in the commercial applications for fibre optics, of course now they're everywhere.

SELF SUPPRESSION

Students here want to graduate so that they can start making money, and do all sorts of things like that. We don't suppress anything. There have been things that could be construed as not very good. Very recently, there were students who were drawing cartoons that were really creative but we were very worried about it . . . But then some other students objected to it, and that took care of it.

Charles Kao

Kao does not regret leaving research management for his present position. He explains that it allows him to deal with the whole field, instead of the relatively narrow area of telecommunications research.

The Chinese University of Hong Kong was founded in 1963. The university has an enrolment

> ## IT ADDS UP
>
> **It's so common that a lot of the
> Chinese are very good at maths.
> All the top maths students are Chinese
> and they hate maths, they don't
> like it but still they score high marks.
> It seems to me, that it might be
> in the genes.**
>
> *Charles Kao*

of around ten thousand students. Initially, university courses were taught exclusively in Chinese; today there is an effort towards bilingualism, and eighty per cent of the textbooks are in English.

Where Wang Gung-wu takes a problem and spreads out an idea that spans continents and generations, Kao's response to a problem is to shrink it to specific actions in which he can participate. One takes a philosophical, the other a practical scientific approach:

> *I am Chairman of an organization called the Technology Review Board. We are looking at the impact of technology on Hong Kong. How do we make good technology investments? How do we approach investment? I am trying to see whether one can take action to help Hong Kong get the most out of technology, and perhaps open up a future industry here.*

We ask him about the impact of 1997 on university administration and curriculum. Kao says that the Basic Law guarantees the university's independence:

> *You can never take anybody's word as gospel. You have to see if they deliver on their word. Nothing makes me suspect that China will kill the goose that laid the golden egg.*

Kao was invited by Beijing to be one of China's Hong Kong advisors. The students were unhappy about his accepting the position, and warned him that he was being used:

> *I said to those students that there is no basic reason for me to doubt the sincerity of the Chinese government to want honest people like myself to be an advisor. The more voices they hear the better. I can definitely speak on technology, and I am happy to do so.*

Charles Kao is closer to Li Ka-shing than he is to Wang Gung-wu. Technology erases borders, and is its own language. Technology and global corporate empires have shifted power from nations into the hands of technocrats and tycoons:

> *The education system is highly culturally sensitive. We are trying to establish multiple contacts with major institutions around the world. We have a programme with Yale University we call the South China Project. It brings us together with dynamic thinkers from Yale. The idea is to address the developmental problems of South China, to see if we can develop some scholarly work that may eventually be of benefit to the region.*

TSUI HARK & NANSUN SHI

Tsui Hark and Nansun Shi are a husband and wife, producer-director, film-making team. Nansun Shi was born in Hong Kong in 1951, and Tsui Hark was born in China in 1950. But their backgrounds and cultural influences are international. They are a fast-moving, fast-talking team. They arrive in a red Porsche convertible, and are dressed head-to-toe in black. They speak over each other's words, not as interpreters, but as an operatic duet.

NANSUN SHI

Her eyes are striking, they are wide open and staring; she dares us to ask questions. She seems fearless. But she is not frightening, it is a girlish bravado from a very sophisticated and intelligent woman. Shi says that it is her ability to be calm in a moment of crisis that made her successful. But she is all nerve, and adrenalin, and words tumble out before fully formed, or thought through:

> *To me Hong Kong was the centre of the universe. But in the 1960s, nobody knew anything about Hong Kong. When I went to boarding school in England they all expected me to do well in maths because I was Chinese. But I was a disaster . . . Slowly, in the late 1960s, I came to feel acutely aware of being Chinese . . . I finished my degree only because I had to, and came back to Hong Kong and started work in a public relations agency.*

She spent a great deal of her time at cocktail parties, which was where you heard who and what was in or out. In the mid-1970s she was hired to host a TV programme on the Miss Universe pageant:

> *The crew wanted to sack the producer, they didn't like him. On the third day, there was a coup d'état. It was my third day in television. The executive producer came around and decided I could do it on my own. It was really just a question of getting the story. I discovered that I had this talent for getting the story if it was there, or staging the thing if there was no story. It went on the air for three weeks so I suppose it was all right.*

THE MESSAGE

In your twenties, you have certain feelings you can't express in a competent technical manner, especially in a script. One of the big set-backs still are the scripts. You know, using that space to tell a story in a certain way and build it up so that it can carry your message.

Nansun Shi

I JUST DID IT

They decided to get me to be the female host of this programme. And through that programme I discovered I had this ability to do simultaneous translation, I had never done it before and I just sort of did it. So for about a year, every weekend I did a special for TV Week, like the Queen's visit to Hong Kong, with simultaneous translation. That was the big thing, sort of live transmission from everywhere.

Nansun Shi

Shi leaps from subject to subject, like a chamois leaping from crag to crag, then delivers a shrewd observation about her own craft:

> *In the late 1970s there was no indigenous culture, it was entirely imported from the West, or dominated by traditional Chinese cultural activities. But Hong Kong started to evolve, and its own indigenous pop culture arrived.*

Shi says that this boom time provided the cash for first-time directors to make their films:

> *They call it now the New Wave, the New Wave movement of Hong Kong. That was when maybe up to fifty directors had their first films made, all within two or three years . . . The interesting thing was that most of the films were more technically competent than we had seen produced here before. Second, the film-makers wanted to send a message; it wasn't just about entertaining. The third thing was that the films were very immature emotionally. And because of that, few of them enjoyed wide popular appeal.*

Of the fifty new voices of the late 1970s only a few remain. Shi says some have become restaurant owners and others have emigrated. Tsui Hark is one of the few still making films today.

Shi says that humour is particularly difficult to do well for a Chinese audience because of traditional Confucian respect for authority. To challenge authority, to humiliate an authority figure, is to run counter to Confucian teachings.

Shi joined a film-making company and found herself among other young and ambitious film-makers. She decided that at best she might become a very good second-rate director. She was also savvy enough to realize she had certain skills the others lacked:

> *I felt I should be the sort of person who creates an environment for these great artists, instead of trying to be a great artist. I think there are very few great artists . . . In the first maybe four years it worked wonderfully, because at the time we were making good money and producing good, solid, wholesome, entertaining films. And there was enough money left over to try some things. In fact, we came to be known as a place where a lot of new film-making took place.*

We asked about the current difficulties in the business, and the cost of production:

> *There might be one or two super productions a year where the budget might be HK $60 million. Then there would be ten or twelve with budgets of $25 million . . . And then smaller*

ones, budgets of $6 or $7 or $8 million, where your brother is the scriptwriter, and your mother the costume person . . . We call them 'brotherhood films'.

We ask Shi about the market for films in China. She says that the opening up of China has allowed film-makers to shoot on location there:

Traditionally, our biggest market for distribution is Taiwan. But Taiwan, because of its relationship with China, always banned films which were made in China, or even that a Hong Kong company might make on location in China. At the moment, you can shoot in China, but your stars, and the talent participating in the film, must be from Hong Kong or Taiwan. If you follow that rule, the film can be released in Taiwan . . . It is impossible to make a film without the support of the Taiwan market . . . China is changing, too. We haven't seen much money yet from distribution in China, it's only US 36 cents a ticket to see a film.

Shi says many film-makers are leaving in anticipation of 1997. But they often end up returning, because they are unable to fit into a foreign, and non-Chinese, environment and culture.

Nansun Shi is cautiously optimistic about how China will treat Hong Kong. She understands that China's population is enormous, and the economy troubled, and says that China will only become freer and more open when it achieves greater political stability. Shi is staying; she also carries a British passport.

TSUI HARK

Tsui Hark was born in Guangzhou and moved to Hong Kong when he was very young. He left Hong Kong in 1968 to study film in the United States:

When I told my family that I wanted to go to America to study film they were shocked. I left Hong Kong and stayed away almost eight years . . . I had seen many films in China when I was young, but the film that moved me, that made me want to make movies, was a simple movie about a swordsman hired by two people in a small village to protect them. It's a sort of Samurai film.

We asked what it was about the film that touched him. He says that he had never seen a film about a Chinese, he had never been able to find himself in any film before that time:

The next day I went to the theatre again to find another film, but the experience was not the same. Eventually, I saw another great film, Akira Kurosawa's The Seven Samurai.

Tsui had wanted to be an architect. After Kurosawa's movie, he turned his attention to film-making, and saw as many different kinds of films as he could. When he finally decided to study the art, he found that the only school that would accept him was in Texas:

America was nothing I had ever imagined. My impressions had come from the movies I had

OPEN DOORS

Television opened its doors to anybody with or without experience. So a lot of this first crop of people who are really now in power in this field all started in television in the middle of the late seventies.

Nansun Shi

seen. Texas meant John Wayne, and a lot of cowboys walking around or riding horses . . . I stayed in Texas for three and a half years and then I went to New York . . . It's sad to say, but nothing I had learned at school was any help to me. I went to work in a film laboratory, and I worked in a newsreel production house. I worked on a newspaper and at a community centre as a social worker.

WORKING-CLASS FILMS

Sir Run Run Shaw's greatest moment in film history in Hong Kong came in the 1960s. Run Run Shaw was the one who single-handedly started the film culture in Hong Kong . . . They made these little films for the masses. Hong Kong's business was manufacturing, so most of these films were about working-class life. Factory workers, they live here, they go there. They were *cinéma vérité* sort of movies.

Nansun Shi

Tsui remembers New York as a difficult time in his life; he was disillusioned and desperate:

> *I almost had to drink gin to keep myself warm, like a wino in the street . . . It was very expensive and I ended up working at a newspaper at night, and at the production house during the day.*

He reached breaking point in New York at the time of the arrest of the Gang of Four in China in 1976. He found himself searching for news of China, and found his friends turning to him for news and opinions on what was going on there. It reminded him of what he had left behind, and that New York would never really be home:

> *So I came back and I wrote letters to three studios and got no reply. So I wrote to Selina Chow. She called me and asked me what I wanted to do. I said I'd do anything. She said, 'But what do you want to do?' I said maybe I want to be a director. She said, 'Okay, so be a director,' and I became a director from that point on. It was that simple.*

He hated his first assignment. It was a television soap opera about three teenage girls. The director had fallen ill, and Tsui was asked to take over. He quickly moved into film but continued to have problems finding good scripts to direct, or script writers to work with. So he wrote a script he was happy with, and shot on location in Taiwan:

> *When I finished, I came back to Hong Kong and I thought I would never make another film. I thought my career was over . . . It wasn't a great success. Neither was my second film. I had total control and I was shooting in Hong Kong. The first one was called* Butterfly Murder, *and the second was called* We Better Eat You. *Neither film worked. I stayed out of film for a year and a half.*

But he persisted, and his fourth effort, *All the Wrong Clues*, was a huge success and established his career.

Tsui founded his own production company in 1984, and named it Film Workshop. The first production was *Shanghai Blues*, a name chosen by Shi:

> *The best way to make a film is to make it according to how you feel, from what you pick up out of the air around you . . . And it's only going to be interesting if you are interesting . . .*

RAYMOND WU

We have arranged our subjects carefully throughout this book. We have clear reasons for grouping them in chapters, and for arranging them in the order they are presented. Why then is Dr Raymond Wu our last subject? Dr Wu is not glamorous, powerful or rich. He does not lead a particularly exciting life, nor is he a brilliant or revered member of his profession. He is ordinary Hong Kong Man. His views, and feelings for his place and time, are probably closer to what the majority feels than anyone else in this book. He is an ordinary man in that he has worked hard and succeeded on his own merits. He is respected in his profession and in the community. He is ordinary but exceptional. He is exceptional because he is engaged in his place and time. But it is cautious engagement. Wu is wary and pragmatic, an odd hybrid of democratic reformer and canny political operative, deep in the bowels of an authoritarian system:

180

> *I don't mind the interview, but honestly, I do not see myself as fitting into any specific place. So I think you can really try to put me in for your own purposes. Use me to understand the whole political situation, the background, the looking forward, all that sort of thing. And then decide where you want to put me, or not at all. I don't mind either way. Honestly speaking, it's up to you . . .*

He is a stocky man. The sound of his voice suggests a man heavier than he is; it is not resonant, it does not rise up from within, it spins off teeth, tongue and lips. He uses specific, and typically Chinese, hand gestures to punctuate his phrases: an index finger pointing to the sky says this is important and true, the flick of a wrist indicates an impatient dismissal.

One's first impression is not quite to trust him. He seems too equivocal. Of course this question never arises from the wealthy and powerful – if only because they are wealthy and powerful. Their money and their connections will always save them. But for most people in Hong Kong, and for Dr Wu, survival depends on placing oneself on the right side, head down and mouth shut, and remembering that the fattest pig is slaughtered first:

ONE COUNTRY, TWO SYSTEMS

They are really trading away Marxism and Communism, all these theories, all the ideology behind it, in order to let Deng Xiaoping's 'one country, two systems' Hong Kong remain a capitalist country. I think that his theory is consistent with that . . . They know that Hong Kong can benefit the modernization of China.

Raymond Wu

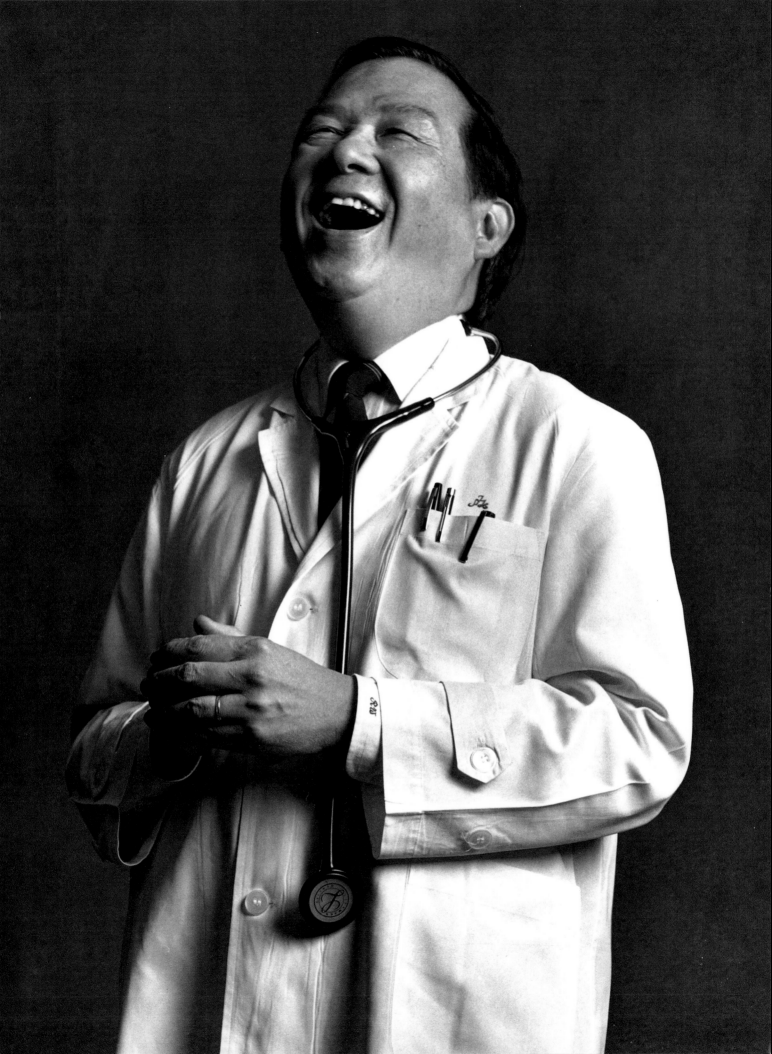

182

THE LAW IS BASIC

I want to make Hong Kong valuable to China. This is number one.
I think the Basic Law is good enough protection, if it can be implemented
one hundred per cent. The worst thing that could happen is a
misinterpretation of the Basic Law. If in the future China is going
to misinterpret it, then I will speak up. As long as the Basic Law is
implemented, we'll be all right. That is the guarantee, the legal guarantee.
But law is for the people who abide and respect the law,
not for people who break the law.

Raymond Wu

I was born in China, in Ningpo, south of Shanghai. My father went from Ningpo to Shanghai to do business. When the Japanese invaded China, he fled to Hong Kong . . . I was educated in Hong Kong. I studied in the Chinese middle school for a while and then switched to English school. So my educational background is all colonial and British. I went to the University of Hong Kong, and went for my postgraduate studies in England. So my training and background is English. So I can perceive what British people are thinking . . . But, on the other hand, I also understand what the Chinese people think, from their culture, background and upbringing.

We asked him about the origin of his community involvement:

My attention was not really active, it was passive . . . It's like my medical practice; I don't choose my patients; if I am given a patient to handle, it is my responsibility to carry through with my duty as a doctor . . . As time went on, I got myself into various community services. Perhaps I sort of demonstrated my ability, and then the government started to appreciate me and recognize me and appointed me to various bodies.

Wu has been active in the community since 1965. He was elected President of the Medical Association in 1984. He says that at first he was sceptical when China asked him to become a member of the Basic Law Drafting Committee in 1985. He was dubious of China's sincerity. When he decided that the Chinese truly wanted Hong Kong to continue to prosper, and that they were consistent in their dealings with him, he devoted more time and energy to the Committee:

I think you must look at Deng's speeches when he spoke on different occasions to Basic Law Drafters . . . He mentioned that 'one country, two systems' is a kind of model for the world to learn from, to settle disputes in a peaceful manner . . . I think, in his mind, he doesn't want anything, but he wants his name to go down in history. 'One country, two systems' might guarantee that.

183

Wu objects when we suggest that China may have a hidden agenda, that what Deng says, and what he intends to do, may be two different things:

That's a Western-style approach. In the West, before you start a business, you do a feasibility study, market research, that sort of thing. But that's not the Chinese way. It's the idea that counts, the concept . . . It's a famous Communist saying, putting a concept into practice is the best way to test it . . . I'm not trying to insist that this is right, but that's what they're doing . . . You can argue with them, but that's how they do things.

Wu argues that the first Chief Executive of the new Hong Kong is likely to be a business leader, because it is business and finance that make Hong Kong valuable to China. He then goes on to say that a civil servant would be a more practical choice, because the purpose of a Chief Executive is to run the government effectively and smoothly, and no one would be more capable of doing that than a senior civil servant. We ask him if China has taken into account Western opinions when making decisions concerning Hong Kong:

I don't think they are concerned at all . . . China just does whatever it likes, they never think of or consider what other people think of what they are doing. This is why Tiananmen happened as it did. They never take into consideration how other people see them.

If China cares little about what the West thinks, what do they think of Hong Kong activists like Martin Lee and Emily Lau?

I think Martin Lee and Emily Lau put them on the alert to think twice about what they're doing. It wouldn't be good if everyone in Hong Kong behaved like a lamb . . . this is the positive side of it. But on the other hand, there is also a negative effect. I think it makes China suspicious and paranoid and might lead to them wanting to tighten up the controls.

Wu says that China is less concerned with pro-democratic activism than it is with anti-China sentiments. He suggests that the Chinese authorities do not object so much to the voicing of dissent among the opposition parties in Hong Kong in general terms as to anything that smacks of a direct attack on authority:

China's objection to these groups is not concerned with the pace of democratization in Hong Kong; it's really the anti-China approach.

THE GREAT EXECUTIVE

**What sort of person, right? What powers does he have
to bargain with the central government? This is the most important thing.
I think to be Chief Executive is easy, if you have a lot of cards. If he
doesn't have a lot of cards, it's very difficult for him.**

Raymond Wu

184

Those who want to push for democracy may be misguided, but those who attack the regime are dangerous, in the eyes of the Chinese, Wu suggests ominously. When asked where he stands, he argues that the key to Hong Kong's ability is for it to remain apolitical:

Whether it is possible is another matter. But that is the ideal situation, the position I advocate. But of course, because we have some elections for the legislature, there will be politics. But that kind of politics, politics that is local, is all right. The danger is including China in those politics, taking the politics into China.

We bring up the question of political succession in China, and the growing concerns over inflation and corruption. We ask if he can possibly be confident in the light of these concerns:

I'm neutral. I wouldn't say I'm confident. I don't know. I think about it, I ask myself the question, but I can't really find the answer. It's all so unpredictable. Well, again, perhaps that's because of my profession. I think my profession has made me cautious of making predictions.

He is brilliantly evasive. He tells us that he is concerned, that he asks himself the hard questions, and gives impeccably rational reasons for not coming to any conclusion that might cause him to act.

Wu is a survivor, and clever enough to know that to be silent and non-committal is no protection at all. But he is not cynical; he is engaged in the political process as much because of his heart as his head. He is a thoroughly admirable and likeable man. Finally, we believe his politics and opinions to be typical of the majority, and his pragmatism, canny ambiguity and caution, the face of 1997 Hong Kong.

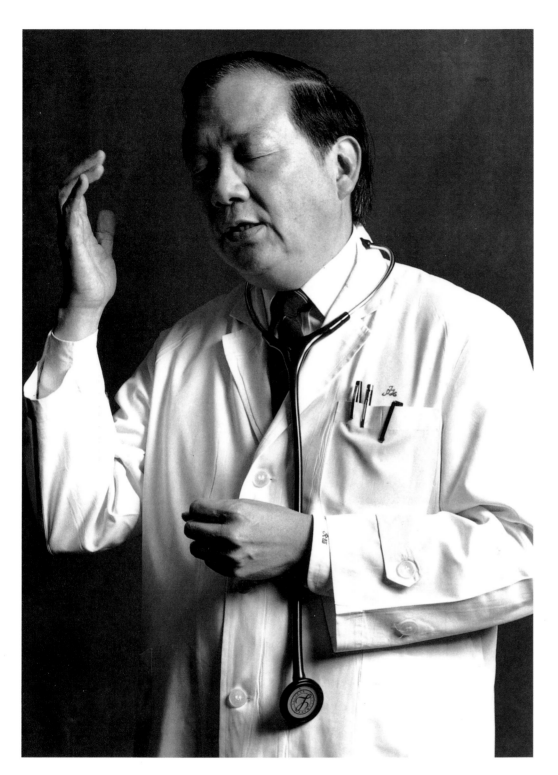

But this will present problems for the rest of the world. How do you support a position that seems ill-defined, and a gambler who always hedges his bets? It is easy to cheer Martin Lee for marching to martyrdom and refusing a blindfold, or side with Cheng Yu-tung who suggests that the welfare state leads to laziness. But these are clichés, and their positions extreme and unpractical. Raymond Wu is something else, and something closer to the truth.

EPILOGUE

I THINK HONG KONG HAS TO CHANGE, AND
CHINA HAS TO CHANGE, BUT I THINK CHINA IS CHANGING
FASTER THAN HONG KONG.
Raymond Wu

186

Hong Kong's civil service and financial institutions have been able to grow so strong in part because they were not attached to the body of any nation. The population was Chinese, but the identity and administration British. A meeting, but not a melding, of races and cultures. As of 1 July 1997 it is Hong Kong, China. It will be labelled a Special Administrative Region, and the administration will appear to function as it did before, but it will be finally and irrevocably tied to the circulatory system of a huge, complex and troubled nation. The inoculation of a treaty and the warm blanket of a foreign flag will no longer protect it from the infirmities of Beijing, or the strained muscles of Guangzhou.

On 1 July 1997, Hong Kong, and the people of Hong Kong – these people, in this book – will be forced to address the central issue of our times. War no longer springs from the clash of ideologies. Perhaps it never did, perhaps democracy, Fascism, National Socialism and Communism were only ever rationalizations for what was at root a tribal or territorial conflict. The fall of the Soviet Union and the civil war in the former Yugoslavia have shown that borders do not define or contain nations. A nation is a union of peoples bound together by culture, race or ideology. Ideology springs from reason and can be dealt with rationally, and like most ideas, has a limited period of relevance. But we have few tools to manage conflicting cultures or races. Our minds and morality tell us we must accommodate to survive, but our guts are tribal and territorial. How will China accommodate Hong Kong? They are the same race, share the same written language, customs and culture. But can they get along? Is there too much lingering resentment on the mainland against these refugees or traitors from China's internal struggles? Can they exchange and benefit from their differences, or must one eliminate what is different in the other to ensure internal stability and confidence in leadership?

187

It is confusing to
learn without thought;
it is dangerous to think
without learning.

The fate of Hong Kong and China rests with Deng Xiaoping's brilliant accommodation – 'one country, two systems'. Can it work? Is it an end in itself, or the means to an end – to fool them only long enough to get them firmly under thumb? It is clear from all of the interviews we did that there may not be time to absorb the reality of the merger before it has taken place. Whatever happens and however it unfolds, it will be different to what anyone expects or can imagine.

We interviewed a group of students to get an idea of how a younger generation and those born and raised in Hong Kong see the situation. We asked Patrick, a young medical student, what he wanted from life, and where he saw himself in five or ten years. His answer was clear and uncomplicated. He said he wanted to graduate, and find work at a hospital, get married, buy a car and a flat, and have two children. We asked him if he was at all worried about 1 July 1997. He told us he didn't think about it much; he wanted to be a doctor and have a family, he wasn't interested in politics. We asked him how he would feel if he received a phone call from Beijing on 1 July 1997, telling him his services were needed in a small village in Mongolia; no roads, no electricity, lovely scenery, fresh air, but not to worry, nothing permanent, ten years only. He paled. He couldn't speak. We twisted the blade. We said everyone tells us Hong Kong has no natural resources, only its people. Why shouldn't Beijing look at Hong Kong's six million as a harvestable human resource? And Patrick would be ripe for picking in 1997. Patrick could not believe, or accept, or take in the implications of what we said. He was in shock, the degree of which made clear that these thoughts had never crossed his mind. This is perhaps the greatest danger to Hong Kong. If you multiply Patrick by six million, shock quickly turns to panic and civil unrest, and Beijing's arm's length becomes a raised club, and the miracle of Hong Kong and the genius of its people a memory.

We began this book with an anecdote about Lord Snowdon and Li Ka-shing. Snowdon swiped the glasses off Li's face, he violated Li's self-image and captured the man himself. We see intelligence in Li's eyes, wary, cautious and quicksilver. We see a body that is compact and erect – conditioned and confident. This is a man comfortable with himself, and confident enough to face anything fate may deliver – including Snowdon's impudent trickery.

Winston Churchill epitomized Western and democratic supremacy in the post-war years. His words, his voice, his body, spoke of the confidence – if not the arrogance – of Western civilization at its peak. He looked like an emperor, the Olympian of youth now grown fat and indulgent, drinking brandy and smoking foot-long cigars. He was on a tour of North America. He told us that an Iron Curtain had fallen between East and West, and a cold war had begun. In Ottawa, Canada, Churchill agreed to a sitting with the Canadian photographer Yosuf Karsh. The result is one of the most remarkable and penetrating portraits of our time. Karsh had asked Churchill to put out his cigar, which delivered clouds of smoke and was a prop for the man, a distraction from his true character. Churchill refused. Karsh was ready to take the picture. He looked into his camera, and then walked back to Churchill as if to straighten a lapel, or brush away a speck of lint, then suddenly reached up and yanked the cigar from Churchill's mouth. He turned and walked back to his camera and took the picture. Churchill, appalled by the effrontery, set his jaw and stares out with all the energy and stubborn determination that helped him survive so many personal and professional catastrophes. He faced all the many obstacles in his path with bulldog determination; his way was right, he would persevere and triumph – not by moral or rational argument – but by force of will.

But that was the time of the great statesmen: Churchill, de Gaulle and Adenauer. Today, corporate power threatens to supersede the power of nations, and men like Li Ka-shing, Rupert Murdoch and Bill Gates hold the floor. How did Li Ka-shing react to losing his glasses? He was not offended, or at least did not show offence; he deferred to the circumstances of the time. He compromised, his boundaries are not so defined and constraining. It was not about standing one's ground, or underlining one's inviolable authority, it was the middle road. He faced Snowdon's impudence and intrusion the way he seems to view the future, with cautious optimism. It was uncomfortable, but not enough to feel threatened and circle the wagons.

Li Ka-shing grew up during Churchill's cold war, and has seen the Iron Curtain fall. His eyes will see a future no one dares to predict. They look out at the world, and at us, with cool, cautious optimism, with a willingness to participate in an unfamiliar process, and an open-mindedness towards change – all the things that made Hong Kong what it is today, and may just determine its future.